# LEAD with NO FEAR

Your 90-day leader shift from
worry, insecurity, and self-doubt to
inspiration, clarity, and confidence

## Steve Gutzler
and
## Mike Acker

To contact, please e-mail: contact@nofearworkshop.com

# Contents

**FOREWORD** BY BOB BURG, BESTSELLING CO-AUTHOR OF THE GO-GIVER .............................................................. 7

**INTRODUCTION** .............................................................. 11

**THE GUIDING PRINCIPLE:** YOUR 3° SHIFT .................. 19
**FIRST SHIFT:** FROM VICTIM TO LEADER ...................... 25
**SECOND SHIFT:** FROM UNAWARE TO SELF-AWARE.. 45
**THIRD SHIFT:** FROM BLACK AND WHITE TO HIGH-DEFINITION ...................................................................... 63
**FOURTH SHIFT:** FROM INSECURE TO CONFIDENT ... 89
**FIFTH SHIFT:** FROM ACTIVITY TO ACCOMPLISHMENT ................................................................................. 109
**SIXTH SHIFT:** FROM SMART TO SMART AND HEALTHY ................................................................................. 129
**SEVENTH SHIFT:** FROM FAST TO FINISHING............. 159

**CONCLUSION**................................................................ 175

**YOUR 90-DAY PLAN TO A-C-T**........................................ 183

**ACKNOWLEDGMENTS**................................................. 197
**ABOUT THE AUTHORS**................................................. 201

*You can succeed if nobody else believes it,*
*but you will never succeed if you don't believe in yourself.*

—William Boetcher


*You are now at a crossroads.*
*Forget your past.*
*Who are you now?*
*Don't think about who you have been.*
*Who have you decided to become?*
*Make it carefully.*
*Make it powerfully.*
*Then act upon it.*

—Anthony Robbins

# FOREWORD BY BOB BURG,
## BESTSELLING CO-AUTHOR OF THE GO-GIVER

The legendary leadership authority, John Maxwell, has often said that "everything rises and falls on leadership."

It seems to me a very accurate statement. Nothing truly productive ever happens until someone casts a vision for that idea, and then they, or someone else, leads the way in bringing that idea to fruition.

In any business, large or small, its entire culture begins with its leadership, and the quality and character of that leadership filters throughout its ranks—whether positive, inspiring, and benevolent; or negative, stifling, and malevolent.

The latter, unfortunately, is a good deal more common, perhaps in part because the former takes a lot more work.

And here is the interesting part: for a leader to effectively provide that kind of powerfully positive leadership, they must first be able to lead themselves.

This takes awareness, acceptance, and a focused, concentrated effort.

If you are that leader, then this is where Steve Gutzler and Mike Acker come into your life.

There is a reason they are both regarded as premiere leadership coaches. Steve and Mike have been in the trenches and know what it takes to lead. What's more, they know how to communicate their message in a clear, understandable, and actionable way that will allow you to make extraordinary gains, and do so relatively quickly.

In fact, the wisdom they share in this fantastic book has proven to help leaders make that all-important shift in just 90 days. Follow their guidance and watch yourself grow in ways you may never have imagined. The result will be a dramatic improvement in your leadership and effectiveness, more respect from those you lead, and the personal sense of happiness that flows from living and leading in a way congruent with your values.

In our current times, especially, the ability to lead in a way that inspires, influences, and ultimately impacts others will make you infinitely more valuable to any group or organization. This book will make an enormously positive difference for you, for those you lead, and for all those whose lives will eventually be touched in the process.

Steve and Mike will help you get there!

*The impossible is often the untried.*
—Jim Goodwin

*The world will belong to passionate, driven leaders...*
*people who not only have enormous amounts of energy,*
*but overcome their fears and energize those whom they lead.*

—Jack Welch

# INTRODUCTION

Collin's company-wide meeting was about to begin. Although he was the Chief Development Officer, was fully prepared, and possessed all of the experience, knowledge, and recognition— he didn't *feel* ready. The title, the experience, and the accolades did nothing to soothe his anxiety. Even though Collin was enormously successful, he was paralyzed by the fear of failure, the fear of falling short, and the fear of being found out as an inadequate imposter.

He found a closet, closed himself inside, and called his mentor and coach, Steve.

*\*\*\**

Susit sat in her corner office. She was only in her twenties, but she had risen, seemingly overnight, to incredible heights as an entrepreneur. Her product is one of a kind and her company provides solutions to small, medium, and large companies. Although she had been confident her entire life, self-doubt was now starting to creep in. There, in her office, she searched the internet for a communication coach and found Mike Acker's website.

She took a deep breath, called Mike, and said, "I have a problem…"

## SOMETHING IS MISSING

You picked up this book, so you can probably relate to these fears on some level. Maybe your position requires you to manage change, or you have an important speech looming, or you are kicking off a new initiative. Perhaps your fear is larger, and you have concerns about how the global market affects your job. Maybe your company has expanded far beyond your dreams. It may be that the attention you receive weighs on you. You are looking for some kind of help by reading this book. You are looking for help in dealing with insecurity, doubt, anxiety, imposter syndrome, insomnia, and concern for your future.

You realize something is missing. You have identified a leadership problem and you are looking for a solution.

Together, we will guide you to lead with no fear. It's not going to occur overnight. Success never happens overnight, but it will happen over time as you purposefully choose to *shift*.

Don't wait until someone else or something else forces you to change. In fact, if you don't feel like you need this book, then *now* is the best time to work through this book. The best time to work on you is when you are doing well. Start today.

*To download the ninety-day plan as a PDF, go to*
https://www.nofearworkshop.com/90-day.

# EXPERIENCE MATTERS

Steve grew up in a family-operated restaurant, where his father modeled personal empowerment and confidence to Steve. This led him to pursue his passion of inspiring personal leaders to greatness. For the last 25 years, Steve has traveled the nation as an in-demand keynote speaker on emotional intelligence and influential leadership, equipping leading organizations and global brands with transformational leadership techniques. He also focuses on executive leadership coaching for C-suite leaders, helping them grow their influence, impact, and inspiration.

Mike has been a public speaker for nearly two decades. The types of speaking engagements have varied through the years, yet one constant has remained: his desire to coach other leaders and communicators. Executive communication coaching increased as the commitment to raising a family slowed down the amount of speaking engagements he agreed to deliver. This shift allows more time to write, develop virtual communication programs, and build his company, ADVANCE.

Together, we have over *fifty years* of experience leading, coaching, and training. Our clients are leaders in corporate America, technology startups, professional sports franchises, medical institutions, government agencies, and higher educational institutions. Our clients come from all sorts of backgrounds, but the results they get have been consistent. We have seen clients make vital shifts that have helped them evolve their leadership and make a significant impact in their field.

We have helped people just like you to speak, to live, and to lead with no fear.

Real-life stories with real-life results fueled the creation of this book. Beyond the official case studies, the names of professionals and some of their details have been changed to protect the identity of well-known leaders and companies. The situations, problems, and feelings, however, are extremely real.

## DON'T LET THIS BE YOUR STORY

Seth Parkens was on a business trip when his heart began to palpitate irregularly. He skipped his normal workout that day and made more health-conscious choices with his diet.

He'd been working long hours. The team packed out the week's schedule with negotiations with key strategic partners. A stereotypical type-A personality, Seth naturally powered through the week, creating incredible plans for his company. But internally, he was wreaking havoc on his body. Seth couldn't seem to calm his heart rate at night.

When the meetings were done, Seth and his team were happy to be flying home. While passing through airport security, though, he stumbled and fell. An attendant took him to the plane in a wheelchair, and his wife was called to meet him when they landed.

Seth was mortified.

He needed help. He couldn't wait another day. His heart yelled at him from the inside, and his wife nudged him from the outside. He'd waited too long, and when he reached out to us, he knew he had to make a change immediately. But what kind of change makes sense for highly driven individuals?

We knew better than to try to change Seth. Instead, we invited him to *shift*. Initially, these shifts felt minuscular, but with his commitment, the end result was massive: Seth became the Chief Information Officer at a leading technology company in the Bay Area. Even more important, he regained balance in his life.

## MINUSCULE TO MASSIVE

We have witnessed incredible transformations of real people experiencing real results:

We promise you that when you begin to shift over the next ninety days, you, too, will see massive results in your leadership.

- You will learn to replace worry, stress, and fear with confident leadership.

- You will be able to clarify your vision.

- You will make a lasting impact on others and inspire them to greatness.

- You will envision long-term life planning.

- You will create a sustainable pace of working toward your goals.

- You will find real joy, while achieving emotional balance, and better health.

## COMMIT TO THIS

We will present seven ways to shift your leadership from fear-based and fear-laced to one of inspiration, clarity, and confidence. We will teach you to do this over ninety days.

Why not commit yourself, your team, and even your entire company to enact this plan for the next quarter? The shifts and actions you need to take are all in this book.

*To simply download the ninety-day plan, go to*
http://nofearworkshop.com/90-day.

*Compound interest is the eighth wonder of the world.*
*He who understands it, earns it ... he who doesn't ... pays it.*

—Albert Einstein


*Do one thing every day that scares you.*

—Eleanor Roosevelt

# THE GUIDING PRINCIPLE:
## YOUR 3° SHIFT

When Captain JJ Cummings, Commander of the World's Largest Aircraft Carrier, commanded the USS Gerald R. Ford to shift direction by three degrees to the right, very few of the 4,550 crew members took notice. Ninety days later, however, when the 1,092-foot-long carrier arrived, crew members realized they'd traveled to a totally different *continent*.

Leadership, in many respects, is like strategically shifting your course, often every ninety days, not in big dramatic announcements or bold claims, but subtle 3° choices and intentional shifts.

In observing and working with hundreds of leaders and organizations in the fields of technology, medicine, government agencies, and in the service industry over a combined fifty years, we've uncovered seven critical *shifts* impactful leaders make to move from a fear-based default leadership style to one that exudes positive influence, sustainable impact, and inspires others to greatness by how they live and lead daily.

We invite you to make subtle changes by illuminating, motivating, and guiding you through the seven strategies. Initially, you may feel that you are not making tremendous headway, but when you begin to employ the 3° shift, you will end up in a completely different destination than where you began.

## ME TO WE LEADER SHIFT

Commander JJ Cummings has thought a lot about his 'captainness' and leadership. On or off the ship, inside and outside the Navy, there are good and bad leaders. There are leaders who instill fear and leaders who inspire confidence. Cummings says, "Poor leaders are focused on their next job or promotion rather than thinking about this as their last job."

We've all seen poor leadership in action. It's short-sighted and insecure, a self-centeredness driven by fear and scarcity. In contrast, the centered and influential leaders serve selflessly. They make sacrifices and drive human potential to soaring new heights in business and non-profit work.

When Cummings attends Change of Command Ceremonies, he plays a mental game: How many times does the commander say, "I or me" instead of "we, our, or us"? Often, the ratio isn't good.

Your leader shifts are not just about you. Simply put, leadership is influence; and you have a shipload of people you are impacting through your daily decisions. Although these shifts are not just about you, they do start with you. As you begin to shift, you will be positively affecting your life and the individual lives of those around you.

*LEADER SHIFTS ARE A 'WE' THING THAT START AS A 'ME' THING.*

# SEVEN SHIFTS TOWARD YOUR 3° DIFFERENCE

1. Shift from Victim to Leader

2. Shift from Unaware to Self-aware

3. Shift from Black and White to High-definition

4. Shift from Insecure to Confident

5. Shift from Activity to Accomplishment

6. Shift from Smart to Smart AND Healthy

7. Shift from Fast to Finishing

*I am not what happened to me,*
*I am what I choose to become.*

—Carl Jung


*A smooth sea never made a skilled sailor.*

—Frank D. Roosevelt

# FIRST SHIFT:
# FROM VICTIM TO LEADER

One of the most significant shifts we can make as a leader is from victim to leader. We're not talking about true victimization but rather a victim *mindset*, victim *self-talk*, and victim *vocabulary*.

## ENCOUNTERING THE DOLDRUMS

**STEVE:** Around 2008, during the Great Recession in the United States, I had slid into my own personal and professional funk of sorts. I like to refer to it as a season; an elongated season of the doldrums.

The doldrums is a nautical term where the inner-tropical convergence zone winds collide and cancel each other out. In ancient days, if sailing ships sailed into the doldrums, they would often drift in circles and never get out. They would die right there unless they received a second wind. I was in the doldrums with my negative and fearful self-talk. My once-optimistic outlook had slipped slowly into cynicism. I started playing the "blame game," accusing others to excuse my own poor behaviors.

That year, my business declined by 45% because the recession was taking a serious toll on my income and my mental health. I was in desperate need of a second wind, but it was nowhere in sight.

Finally, it came in the form of a phone call from Jim, a long-standing friend and client. He said, "Steve, I'd like to invite you to speak in August at my team's first integral rafting and kayaking trip for at-risk teens. As you know, I have a summer rafting business and I'd like to dedicate one week to non-profit, experience-based inspiration. We will kayak down the Rogue River, camp at night, and I'd love for you to speak to teens at risk to motivate and inspire them."

## FROM OBLIGATION TO OPPORTUNITY

When you are in a negative funk and in the doldrums, you often look at life through a lens of obligation, not opportunity. I only heard two things from that conversation: camping and at-risk teens. I don't like to camp, and working with teenagers can be challenging (yet rewarding when in a funk).

I said, "Yes!" because I felt obligated.

Two weeks before the trip, Jim called me and said they couldn't pull off getting the teen group together, but instead they confirmed over 30 young adults... burn victims from Oregon State Burn Institute. I was to meet Jim in the Emmanuel Hospital Burn Unit parking lot and then we would take a four-hour bus ride to the Rogue River to spend the week together. "Steve, they have your bio information and are very excited to hear you speak," Jim said.

I'll never forget greeting the first woman that morning. She was a beautiful, dark-haired young lady with a deep red scar across her face. Just like her, all these brave souls had burns on 30% to 95% of their bodies.

As we drove those four hours to the river, I heard amazing and heartbreaking stories about victims who were burned in a backyard accident, trapped in a burning car following an accident, and injured from stove-top explosions. One person had even survived an airplane crash.

The first day on the river was my second wind because I heard nothing but positivity, laughter, joy, and "can do" spirit of these young adults. I witnessed people pulling together with cheers of encouragement. I stood that night to speak and my voice cracked as I said, "I came here in a little bit of a funk, but watching and observing each of you has truly inspired me." Then I paused and continued, "Can I be honest? I've never been around burn victims and didn't know what to expect."

Within seconds, a young man with a prosthetic arm lifted his hand. "With all due respect, Mr. Gutzler," he said, "we don't refer to ourselves as victims. We are burn survivors."

## VICTIM TO SURVIVOR

*Burn survivors.* That statement took my breath away. I learned that the incredible medical staff, physical therapists, and support groups at Oregon State Burn Institute are very intentional about referring to patients as survivors, not victims. The evening following my talk, I went back to my cabin to write in my journal with a new inner dialogue, self-talk, and vocabulary. I would no longer allow victim talk in my mind. I would only speak the language of the leader, not the victim.

## LEADERSHIP LANGUAGE

I wrote in my journal the difference between victim and leader:

- Victims talk about what they hate, leaders talk about life and love

- Victims talk about their problems, leaders talk about their opportunities and solutions

- Victims talk about what tires them, leaders talk about what inspires them

- Victims talk about their past, leaders talk about their present and future

- Victims talk about what broke their heart, leaders talk about what opens their heart

- Victims talk about things in life that aren't working, leaders talk about things that are working

- Victims talk about being victims, leaders talk about surviving and thriving

How about you? Take a moment and consider the audio track playing inside your mind. Does it empower you daily, or does it disrupt your behaviors and beliefs? What elimination words (words you would like to remove from your vocabulary) sabotage your leadership and successful outcomes? Are you attracting others with the language of leadership or repelling others with the language of victimhood?

We attract what we project. Now is the time for strong self-talk and an empowering language that attracts others to you.

## FEAR LEADS TO VICTIMHOOD

Leadership often focuses on what we do, but when confronted with fear, action can seem impossible. Leadership learning needs to start with the heart.

When the economy takes a downturn, when initiatives don't work, when feedback is filled with negativity, when quarterly returns steadily decline, or when pressure and expectations mount, then we don't need another thing to know or do, we need a new way to think. These external circumstances force us to put on dark-colored glasses. When circumstances cause fear to increase, our worldview darkens. This sets off a downward spiral: such circumstances lead to negative self-talk, which leads to seeing more fearful circumstances, which leads to more self-doubt, which leads to doubting even the goodness around us, which leads to insecurity, which leads you into the leadership doldrums...

## WHAT OTHERS SAY

**MIKE:** When I was a freshman in high school, I encountered a negative external circumstance every day: an 18 year old bully who waited for my arrival and cussed me out. His cruel words started to make their way inside my mind and they took root and shape there. Some evenings I would sit in my room thinking only about how much my life sucked. Feeling despondent, I'd listen to Pearl Jam cassettes in my boombox, over and over. Eddie Vedder sang *"how much difference does it make"*. And my favorite song to rewind and repeat was titled *Black*.

Fear of not fitting in led to victimhood, which created negative self-talk, which led to finding other reasons for not being happy, which led to listening to somber music, which led to thinking depressing thoughts, creating more self-doubt... I was trapped in my own mind.

Thankfully, a retreat that summer disrupted my environment. I met a mentor who challenged me to shift my thinking through affirmations, reading, and rehearsing. The exercises my mentor gave me didn't take much time, but they redirected my thinking. I gradually shifted from thinking like a victim to thinking like a leader.

*** 

We can easily trap ourselves in a downward spiral. We can act like teenage Mike or camp-resistant Steve. But we don't have to. We can shift our thinking to reflect true leadership: influencing the people around us to experience a better reality.

# CHANGE YOUR INTAKE

To shift toward confidence in your leadership, you need to shift away from the track your mind plays on loop.

### *CHANGING YOUR INPUT CHANGES YOUR OUTPUT.*

As a leader, you need to know the real circumstances. In *Good to Great,* Jim Collins offers compelling data showing that leaders must face the brutal facts. Pretending that problems don't exist does not display confidence. Avoidance is not courage, it is cowardice. Jim Collins rightly encourages leaders to accept reality. He aptly titled his fourth chapter: "Confront the Brutal Facts (Yet Never Lose Faith)."

### *REMEMBER: AVOIDANCE IS NOT COURAGE, IT IS COWARDICE.*

Be aware of the external circumstances, but don't let them dictate your inner dialogue. No one can write that dialogue other than you. You are the author of the script that you speak to yourself.

What do you need to do to change the intake of your mind?

# CASE STUDY: STEVE BODE

Steve Bode was a successful businessman near Los Angeles. The terrorist attacks and economic fallout of 9/11 led Steve to close his business. He decided to start over. He discovered a business niche, and developed a brand new business servicing car dealerships. He worked hard and long and finally saw success. Soon after, the steady cash flow made Steve comfortable but also complacent. He became distracted, and one of his partners took advantage of his trust and nearly ruined the business.

Years of hard work were upended. Steve Bode grew despondent and discouraged and developed a victim mindset. This was extremely odd because he has *always* been positive and upbeat. But the thing about a victim mindset is that it can happen to anyone. And Steve realized that it had happened to him.

Steve told us, "I took a good, hard look at my life. I always felt that I had a lot of potential, and at the time really thought I was doing the right things to get the kind of life I wanted. And to some degree, I was, but I was also doing a lot of things that were pushing me backward, or at best, weren't moving me forward. I wasn't taking very good care of myself, which reduced my energy, and I was wasting a lot of time and effort doing meaningless things, like watching TV. Once I realized that I had allowed myself to get stuck, I decided to do something about it."

How do you get out of a profound rut?

*YOU INTENTIONALLY AND COURAGEOUSLY CONFRONT REALITY AND SHIFT DIRECTIONS.*

# STEVE BODE'S 3° SHIFT

Steve began to do some small exercises every morning. Every day, he added one repetition to his growing routine. As he grew more physically fit, he began to listen to audiobooks during his workout. Soon he was listening to a few audiobooks each week. He changed his routine and his input.

The audiobooks put new thoughts in his mind. One of the books encouraged the reader to hire an executive coach. Steve acted on the advice and reached out to Mike. With new guidance, Steve began to climb out of his rut. He reorganized and rebranded his business. His profits tripled in the first year after making the shift from victim to leader.

Those 3° shifts were gradual. Doing ten push-ups doesn't produce instant results, but adding one to the routine over time does. Over the course of a year, Steve performed 200 body weight repetitions daily, finished more than 52 audiobooks, rebranded his business, launched an app (aimed at helping people shift), published his first book, and developed a proprietary investment system.

*WORK OVER TIME PRODUCES RESULTS.*

All of Steve's external success started with an internal shift. Everything good or bad starts internally. A shift in mindset can change a life.

# TO SWITCH YOUR SCRIPT

## 1. Choose your News.

At the writing of this chapter, the Coronavirus has spread across the globe. Currently, Coronavirus accounts for the majority of the headlines. Just before restaurants closed to limit exposure, we sat together at a table in Wood's Coffee in Bellevue, Washington. We discussed the timeliness of creating content about overcoming fear during the panic caused by the pandemic. And this brings up a strategic suggestion: choose your *news*. This may be official news headlines or it may be following stocks, inundating your mind with social media, or listening to naysayers. Be careful what you fill your mind with.

*READING THE NEWS AND WATCHING THE NEWS TRANSLATES INTO FEELING THE NEWS!*

Consider heeding the wise advice of Chandler Bolt, CEO of Self-Publishing School:

> *"Don't read the news first thing in the morning or last thing in the evening. Instead, choose positivity in the morning and evening. Start your day and end your day with faith, hope, and inspiration. Your day can easily fill up with disheartening news and discouraging returns. Be aware of what is happening around you, but limit your exposure."*

## 2. CHANGE YOUR MUSIC.

Leadership guru, John Maxwell, discourages listening to music while driving. He argues that we have a limited amount of time to read books on leadership, growth, and development. Instead of listening to music, he advocates for filling your mind with audiobooks and podcasts.

Personally, we do both. We enjoy music (Mike still spins vinyl Pearl Jam records at home in his library). We also monitor our intake to ensure that we are listening to more leadership encouragement than entertainment. In difficult times, we lean into uplifting sources. Whenever we're tempted to think like victims, we intentionally change the messaging and even the music.

## 3. CHALLENGE YOURSELF.

You might choose to surround yourself with positive influences, to choose the news, to change your music and yet, even then, we acknowledge that you may *still* give in to negative self-talk from time to time.

We obviously believe in the value of hiring coaches to help shift patterns of thinking. Yet, to shift from victim to leader, *you* must constantly challenge yourself. Write out and rehearse powerful affirmations. Look yourself in the mirror and will yourself to greater heights. Keep a journal and record your progress. Challenge yourself to lead with no fear.

\*\*\*

**MIKE:** As a young twenty-year-old entrepreneur, I attended a workshop by Jeanne Mayo. Jeanne has led multiple nonprofit ventures and has established a brand of raising up young leaders who work with students. In her 70s, she continues to speak and work with young people.

In the workshop I attended, she lamented that teenagers often didn't see the value in her leadership. We smiled and nodded as we understood her sentiment (many of us volunteered with youth organizations). She offered the most corny, and utterly profound suggestion: "When no one is around you to encourage you and challenge you, you have to challenge yourself. So raise your hand in the air—come on, do it—make a mouth with your hand and turn it to face you. Then use your hand as a puppet and make it say, 'You can do this, I believe in you.'"

The whole room laughed.

But we raised our hands in the air and used our hands to challenge ourselves. It was cheesy. It was silly. It was brilliant.

I have put my hand up and used my puppet hand to challenge myself many times.

(Steve has also challenged himself many times, but he doesn't use his hand as a puppet.)

# SUGGESTED SCRIPTS

As you examine your mindset, be inspired by poet *Arthur Ward* who suggested a different way of thinking and acting:

- Believe while others are doubting

- Plan while others are playing

- Study while others are sleeping

- Decide while others are delaying

- Prepare while others are daydreaming

- Begin while others are procrastinating

- Work while others are wishing

- Listen while others are talking

- Smile while others are frowning

- Commend while others are criticizing

- Persist while others are quitting

- Save while others are wasting

Keeping in line with Arthur Ward, we have differentiated how individuals embrace a fear-based leadership mentality versus learning how to lead with no fear:

| Fear-Based Leadership Mentality: | Lead with No Fear Mentality: |
| --- | --- |
| That step is way too aggressive | We have the solutions |
| We don't have finances or resources | Problems fuel innovation |
| The deadline is too aggressive | We will change the landscape |
| Last time we tried, we failed | We are ready for the challenge |
| It's a waste of energy | Think of the amazing opportunity |
| Our clients won't buy it | Let's think big and what's possible |
| We don't have the expertise | Let's lead the way |
| Our team couldn't pull that off | Let's re-allocate our resources |
| We don't have the technology | We might be lean, but we are hungry |
| Things will not improve | Let's network and find great people |
| Let the competition try it | Let's show the critics they are wrong |
| It's too bold | Let's take a calculated risk |
| Our team is not up for it | People will love it and purchase it |
| We simply can't | Yes, we can! |

# SWITCH THE WORDS YOU SPEAK

| Begin to eliminate these words: | Choose to these words instead: |
|---|---|
| • I can't | • I can |
| • If only | • I will |
| • I don't think | • I know |
| • I don't have time | • I will make time |
| • Maybe | • Absolutely |
| • I'm afraid | • I'm confident |
| • I don't believe | • I do believe |

Maybe last year was tough. Maybe *right now* is full of uncertainty and overwhelm. This may be the perfect time to be more intentional with your mindset and words. Remember that you are not a victim. You are a survivor. You will get through this. You will survive. You will shift, and over time, you will ultimately thrive again.

That pain does not define you, but it can be a part of the story.

## STEPS TO SHIFT

You will never rise above these two things in life and leadership:

1.  Your self-concept: how you see yourself, your self-esteem, your personal worth and value

2.  Your self-talk and your chosen vocabulary

As you analyze your inner-dialogue and the words you often speak, keep these four strategies at the forefront of your thinking:

1.  *Decide* the type of words that will best influence you and keep you positive.

2.  *Defend* yourself against words that hold you back or create a victim mindset.

3.  *Design* a powerful self-talk list of mantras and say them out loud every day.

4.  *Determine* that words matter. Be positive, optimistic, and full of faith.

# LEADER-SHIFT QUOTES

*"People don't want to be managed, they want to be inspired and led."*—Steve Gutzler

*"What you invest your time and energy in will define who you are."*—Mike Acker

*"We cannot manage time; we can only manage our thoughts, energy, and actions."*—Steve Gutzler

*"Busyness is rooted in one thing: saying yes too often to things you should say no to."*—Mike Acker

*"Your goal should be to spend your days on MVPs (most valuable and profitable work and relationships)."*
—Steve Gutzler

*"Success in any endeavor is a result of two things: focused time and being present."*—Mike Acker

*"If past failures slow you down or consume your thoughts, then failure is a trap that steals time from today."*
—Steve Gutzler

*"Few quality relationships are far more valuable and less time-consuming than many shallow ones."*
—Mike Acker

*"Don't let fear steal your future. We are designed for something more. Something more fulfilling, more rewarding, more enriching, more exciting, and much more significant."*
—Steve Gutzler and Mike Acker

*Some leaders are uncomfortable with expressing emotions
about their dreams,
but it's the passion and emotion that will attract and motivate
others.*

—Jim Collins

*The two most important days in your life are the day you were
born and the day you find out why.*

—Mark Twain

## SECOND SHIFT:
# FROM UNAWARE TO SELF-AWARE

**MIKE:** Antonio was on a successful career track. At thirty-four, he interviewed for the position of principal at a large school. He felt prepared when the interview came, and after the interview, he was confident he had done well... until he received a phone call from his friend.

Antonio's friend was connected to one of the board members who attended the interview. Through his friend, he learned that his performance at the interview was not well-received. The board thought Antonio was boring and arrogant. One of the members simply remarked, "I just didn't like his voice." Antonio's friend was able to convince the board to offer him a second interview based on their positive relationship, as well as Antonio's accomplishments.

Antonio searched for a coach and began to work with me. Once I understood the interview dynamics, I asked him to do a mock interview with me using the questions he recalled from his first interview, and I recorded this coaching session. After the mock interview, I asked Antonio to evaluate his own performance. He noted a few small areas in need of improvement. I said, "Antonio, I want you to succeed, and I hope you will listen to my candid feedback. Then I want you to watch the recording of your interview. Work on the feedback you get today and come prepared for our next session."

I didn't hold back on anything in my feedback because I knew how important this interview was for him.

I described why the board would have drawn their conclusions: his mannerisms hinted at arrogance, his messaging repeated itself, his tone of voice bored the listener, he used fillers, and his style of speaking distanced him from his audience. I could tell it was hard for Antonio to hear my feedback. However, good leaders lean in even when it hurts, and Antonio is a leader. He pushed back on a few areas and made excuses for others. After a spirited debate, though, Antonio committed to watch the recording.

At our second coaching session, it was evident that Antonio had been working on implementing my feedback. He watched the recording from our first session. Seeing his mistakes embarrassed and enlightened him. He became aware of what the board had seen. Without argument, he committed fully to the second session.

During the next interview, the board was impressed by his enthusiasm, coherence, and engagement. Though Antonio did not get the role he applied for, in the end he received an even better position.

*INCREASED AWARENESS LEADS TO AN INCREASE IN SUCCESS.*

# THE LETTUCE IN THE TEETH MOMENT

Every single reader has had a 'lettuce in the teeth' moment. You know, when you have the salad for lunch and the salad stays with you for the rest of the day? Then you get in the car to drive home for the day, and while checking the mirror you see it: a huge piece of lettuce covering the entirety of a front tooth. You quickly dislodge the green glob while reliving the second half of the day: the meeting you had, the interactions with others, and the trip to the barista. Quickly, you count how many people saw what you didn't see and said nothing.

Coaches are "there is lettuce in your teeth" people. We will say it kindly, humbly, and directly. Our philosophy is that it is better to hear the truth from a friend than laughter from others. Therefore, as we come to this second shift, we have something to tell you:

There is lettuce in your teeth.

In other words, there is something that others see in you that you have yet to see.

After you have a truly embarrassing 'lettuce in your teeth' moment, you'll begin to shift your habits. You may go to the restroom mirror after every lunch meeting. You might put a toothbrush in your office. Or you may simply do a quick check in your car. Once it happens to you, you make a shift so it doesn't happen again.

# FEAR OF THE KNOWN

Many would-be-leaders fear knowing what they don't know. They hope that no one points out the lettuce even if the lettuce is obviously right there (and has been there for a long time!) These types of leaders want to look good, feel good, and only hear good things. They don't understand how easily that translates into bad outcomes. These types of people are scared to hear the bad.

To some measure, every single person fears bad news. We fear news about the loss of loved ones, the negative feedback about our work, and comprehending the severity of a pandemic. Like Antonio, we don't want to hear critical feedback even when we know we need to hear it. We are wired to crave positive reinforcement for our performance.

Plus, news that is more personal and emotional is more heavily weighted. It's easier to hear that we didn't perform a function well than to hear that we didn't treat a person well. It's easier to hear that we lack training than to hear that we lack empathy.

When we work with leaders on 360° Leadership Assessments, we help them see the positive and acknowledge the negative. We help them become aware of what others see: positive, neutral, and negative, of both the professional and personal.

It's fascinating how these assessments often reveal issues of emotional intelligence versus technical intelligence and IQ.

# BLINDSPOT AND POTENTIAL LIABILITIES

**STEVE:** I was recently asked to work with executives in a government agency to improve their emotional intelligence and leadership. All leaders were highly trained in the technical aspects of managing teams and executing results:

- Vision and clarity

- Strategy and objectives

- Execution and goals

- Finance and budgets

- Technology and Innovations

However, they were lacking in their ability to lead with emotional intelligence, and these aspects had become a liability… a glaring blindspot:

- Self-awareness of emotional influence

- Emotional self-management under stress

- Emotional management of others

- Communication and effective collaboration

- Building rapport and connections

# USE THEIR OWN DATA

My first training focused on increasing their self-awareness as leaders. In the session I asked them to list three leaders who had directly influenced them and impacted their leadership in positive ways. Along with asking them to write down these people's names on a post-it note, I also asked them to write down the primary characteristic of their leadership. Then, on a large white board, I labeled three columns:

| Technical Competencies | IQ Skills | Emotional Intelligence |
| --- | --- | --- |

I asked the leaders to review the primary characteristic they'd written down and to stick their post-its under the corresponding category on the white board. As usual, perhaps only two or three post-its landed in the Technical Competencies or IQ Skills categories. The white board was overwhelmingly filled with leaders possessing high levels of emotional intelligence. Their qualities included Listening, Motivating, Empowering, Open Communication, Team Building, Empathy, Inspiration, Authenticity, Great Coaching, Trusted Mentorship, Adaptability, Flexibility, Confidence, Optimism, Resiliency, and Personal Drive.

With this exercise, it became obvious that the leaders who inspired greatness were leaders with high levels of emotional self-awareness.

Each of the managers expressed amazement at their own data. They had recently taken and reviewed their own Leadership 360° Assessments and discovered *blind spots* and *potential liabilities* to their leadership; many of which fell into the *Emotional Intelligence* column. They each needed to shift from unaware to self-aware to lead with no fear.

## CASE STUDY:
# DR. COLLEEN MURRAY, PHD, LPC

Clients, conferences, and courts seek out Dr. Colleen Murray for her counsel in high-conflict custody issues. She has developed a reputation for maintaining a calm composure in extremely intense situations. Dr. Murray admits, however, that in an earlier life, she'd displayed the complete opposite. When we interviewed Dr. Murray, she shared her secret of transforming from volatile to calm. She credits four shifts of self-awareness.

Colleen grew up in the 1970s in a hostile environment. She lived in the projects; her family lacked financial resources and didn't provide her with a safe space. Tragically, she was mugged twice before she was even six years old, and she was molested as a child.

Colleen worked hard to fit in at school. Every year, this became harder as she fell behind on her reading skills. She began to think of herself as dumber than the other kids in her class.

At the start of fifth grade, her teacher noticed her struggle with reading. Instead of just correcting her mispronunciation, he took the time to understand her struggle. With his attention and instruction, Colleen became aware of her learning disability (input dyslexia) and how to grow through it. This was her first shift.

But Colleen's struggle to learn and to fit in would plague her throughout her education. After high school, Colleen skipped college to start working. For nine years, she worked hard, performed well, and lived well. Until one day, she came to her second revelation. She had reached her maximum earning potential with the skills she possessed. She needed to find a better path.

At twenty-seven years, Colleen applied to many colleges and universities to get an education, but without a strong GPA or financial backing, her numerous applications were rejected. Except for one. Colleen was finally accepted into a college where she courageously confronted her fears of inadequacy. She shifted a third time.

Colleen enlisted in the military to help pay for her education. She was a quick study of the "politics" of the military, and she rapidly moved up in rank. As she advanced in leadership, she embarrassed herself on numerous occasions. Once, as a Lieutenant, she held up an entire company of Privates when she couldn't initially force herself to make a tower jump. Eventually, the Sergeant forced her to jump by booting her in the backside. She decided that she would choose to confront fear on her own instead of being forced to by another.

As a Captain, a fourth shift took place. She told us, "In 2003, my emotional intelligence significantly advanced. I was in an abusive relationship then with my first husband and I developed a heightened awareness of how I communicated with him. It was during this time that I became aware of the space I took up physically, spiritually, and emotionally. Up until this point, I didn't realize how reactive I was. I would either cuss you out or cut you off. Because I was married to an abuser, I had to learn to respond, and not react. Responding is crafting a considered and choreographed response. Reaction is what immediately springs to mind. I had to learn to self-regulate to be able to respond."

In the military and through marriage, she realized that she had an incredible ability to read people. Yet, she still fought her insecurities of not being smart enough. She said, "I didn't realize I was smart enough until I realized my talents. Figuring out what made me unique is how I gained confidence and became creative. I realized that I could hear what people were saying and what they weren't saying. I could hear their pain, their doubt, their fear, and that they were wanting to tell me something that they weren't actually saying with their mouths."

With this growing understanding, Colleen pursued her master's degree in counseling and eventually achieved her doctorate in the Philosophy of Mental Health.

Dr. Murray lives a life of growing awareness. This awareness quells her fear, elevates her leadership, and she brings inspiration and healing to others.

# EMOTIONS INFLUENCE EMOTIONS

Leaders need to recognize their emotions to understand how they influence the emotions of others. Leaders who are self-aware manage the mood of their organization. They read and regulate their own emotions while intuitively understanding how others feel. They maintain their organization's emotional state as a whole.

If you are incredibly gifted and smart, you can cover for an absence of self-awareness and emotional intelligence until:

- There is an unexpected crisis (i.e. COVID-19)

- Crap hits the fan (AKA, a large client exits and aligns whole-heartedly with the competition)

- Things get really tough in business (key members of your team move on)

At that point, you won't have built up the social capital needed to drum up the best of yourself and your people under tremendous pressure.

Shifting from an unaware to self-aware leadership style inspires others to produce exceptional work. High IQ or technical expertise alone is insufficient and falls flat under pressure.

Self-awareness as the cornerstone competency of emotional intelligence can be learned and improved. A 3° shift can often show substantial results in how people respond and work with you. Data shows that people's self-awareness tends to increase with age. Recognizing your moods, attitudes, and emotions can and will influence those you lead.

One of the common complaints we hear from team members is how their manager's default emotions (negative and stress-filled) create a toxic environment. Often, the core problem is that managers excelled at being individual contributors. However, being a solo star doesn't teach you the skills of persuasive influence, leading, and inspiring others.

# BLIND SPOTS

To begin your subtle shift from unaware to self-aware, there are three strategies to learning about your leadership blind spots:

## 1. INFORMATION.

You will need candid assessments of your strengths and limitations as a leader from colleagues, peers, and team members who know you well and whose opinions you trust. We can partner with you and your team with our:

*Lead with No Fear 360° Assessment*
reach us at contact@nofearworkshop.com

## 2. COACHING

The coaching you need is a specific leadership development plan that uses real workplace encounters and scenarios as a laboratory for learning and improving your leadership skills. Make sure to focus on developing self-awareness skills with actionable goals.

Such types of coaching include executive leadership, executive presence, high performance and life coaching, programs, schooling, and a trusted boss-employee relationship.


## 3. SUPPORT

You will need a peer to share ideas with and to discuss how to handle different situations, especially when you're under stress or managing a challenging relationship. It's important to gain support to stay on track when you might otherwise judge too quickly, or overreact as the stress hormone cortisol emotionally hijacks your rational brain response.


# SELF-AWARENESS

*self-a·ware·ness*

noun:

1. conscious knowledge of one's own character, feelings, motives, and desires.

If you cultivate these resources and begin practicing higher levels of self-awareness, you will experience positive results and attract higher levels of business, income, and influence. *Self-awareness* is the most important emotional intelligence competency to develop. When you grow the self-awareness aspect of your emotional intelligence, you will inevitably grow your bottom line.

It's exciting and fulfilling to partner with extraordinary people in leading technology companies and government agencies and to witness the transformation of leaders dedicated to growth. We've seen leaders learn to calm themselves down under pressure. We've seen them learn to crave constructive feed-forward advice. We've seen managers become aware of the contagious nature of emotion and go on to create positive working environments for others to thrive in, become happier, and perform at their very best.

## DAVID'S 360° BREAKTHROUGH SHIFT

Having served as CEO for over five years, David was ready to "take his leadership influence to the next level." He agreed to participate in a 360° Feedback Listening Tour with his board, his six direct reports, and two important and trusted strategic partners.

He was already running a successful organization that was "on point" with vision, business strategies, and execution. The organization already received good feedback from stakeholders. Revenue was solid. There was just one nagging issue: In moments of authentic discussion around his leadership, trusted team members confided in David that he lacked self-awareness.

We collected data from the assessments and we averaged out the scores of his leadership skills and competencies. We reviewed the responses to open-ended questions, gathering earnest and honest feedback. We asked what was the one big piece of advice they would give David to grow his leadership influence, impact, and inspiration.

## TWO DEVELOPING LEADERSHIP SKILLS

David scored well in over 85% of the feedback. The two developing skills we discovered that he could work on were:

1. *Listening Skills: being an active listener and listening in order to get the best advice and information; and asking follow up questions.*

2. *Emotional Impact: Realizing his emotions were transferable and that they set a tone for the whole organization.*

David took this feedback to heart. He wasn't defensive. He asked if we could create a method for him to become more self-aware and to increase his active listening skills. We defined 12-16 actionable goals to increase his skills, gain real-time feedback and to become a world-class listener. He would be able to answer the question: "How am I improving?"

David also set action goals for increasing positive emotions as a leader. These included developing positive body language, smiling more, creating ease, and displaying upbeat moods that could be transferable to the team. If positive emotions primed better performance, he would set a new intention each day: "What emotion am I transferring to my organization today?"

Within weeks, people could see and sense the change in David.

## SHIFT:
# INCREASE YOUR EMOTIONAL INTELLIGENCE

### 1. GET ACTIONABLE FEEDBACK

In a study of stock performance of 48% publicly traded companies, Korn Ferry International found that companies with strong financial performance tend to have leaders with higher levels of self-awareness than poorly performing companies.

How do you increase self-awareness? Feedback. Honest, actionable feedback helps you as a leader to understand the impact of your emotions on others. Uncover these two or three blind spots that hold you back from your best leadership and performance! With greater awareness comes better choices, and with better leadership choices come far better results and performance.

### 2. IDENTIFY EMOTIONAL TRIGGERS

Do you know your emotional triggers? We all have a tendency to overreact to certain people, events, or actions. To get started, choose a trigger you know you're reacting to poorly (in a way that has a negative impact on your desired outcomes) and come up with a proactive, positive response you'd like to replace it with.

For example, you might have a team member who excels at pointing out the negative. This triggers you to react authoritatively which shuts down potentially helpful collaboration. Instead of letting yourself get triggered by negative feedback, consider choosing to ask three probing questions. This gives your team the chance to dive into the issue and it gives you the chance to calm your frustration.

Know that your triggers can serve as "warning lights" to slow down and play at your best.


## 3. TURN FAILURE INTO A FRIEND, COACH, AND MENTOR

Rather than beat yourself up, learn from leadership mistakes and mishaps. Turn these emotional intelligence discoveries into coaching moments for improvement.

One client recently shared how she had cut someone off at an all-hands retreat because they were dragging on a bit too long with their PowerPoint briefing. Although everyone in the room was a bit relieved, it caused emotional damage to this young manager. Later, she publicly apologized for the interruption, noting that her manager was doing an outstanding job and that the hard work was appreciated. "I was too impatient, and that was on me, not you," she explained.

These kinds of victories build trust and respect among those you influence. They model centered leadership, humility, and a service to others that elicits loyalty.

*When you look into the future, it should be so bright it burns your eyes.*

—Oprah Winfrey

*Good business leaders create a vision, articulate the vision, passionately own the vision, and relentlessly drive it to completion.*

—Jack Welch

## THIRD SHIFT:
# FROM BLACK AND WHITE TO HIGH-DEFINITION

**STEVE:** Often, when conducting a full-day workshop, I ask: "How many of you here can remember black and white televisions?" Sometimes I'll receive a blank stare and polite chuckles, but I'm always encouraged when I receive a scattering of hands raised.

We had a color television when I was a child, but my grandparents had a black and white television. When we were first married, my wife Julie and I received a hand-me-down television. It was only 13 inches. But beggars can't be choosers! I imagined that someday we'd be able to upgrade to a 24-inch and then a 35-inch Sony.

It's funny how our dreams and goals change with time. I dreamed of getting a 35-inch television, but just a few years back, when we hit the "big time", we purchased a large, 54-inch flat-screen TV.

**MIKE:** Ironically, I've used this same opening in presentations! I grew up in a television-resistant family. My dad very rarely watched it, and my mom only watched classic movies she loved with Cary Grant, Humphrey Bogart, and Audrey Hepburn.

Although our television was a color model, it seemed always set to black and white! Whenever I went over to a friend's house and saw a large screen in color, I was shocked because I was so used to seeing it in black and white!

## GLARING DEFICIENCY

When it comes to leadership, people often don't have *high-definition* vision for where they can end up. They often can't even imagine that it can be better than *black and white*!

In working with hundreds of leaders and with organizations over our combined 50 years, we have discovered a glaring deficiency: many leaders lack absolute clarity of vision. Many leaders are stuck. Why is that? Why can't they see past the black and white vision of the past?

Many leaders are so busy triaging the daily crises, focused on the urgent deadlines, that they've lost sight of what they want to accomplish in their personal and professional lives with absolute clarity. They can't picture who they are becoming as leaders.

## BIG QUESTION

Here's our big question: As you read (or maybe listen to) this book, *Lead With No Fear*, ask yourself this: how clear is your vision of the future? What kind of 'TV' are you looking at? Are you settling for black and white when you could have a high-definition TV? Are you imagining a 20-inch when you could upgrade to a 54-inch or 72-inch or even 98-inch?

Are you limiting yourself? When it comes to your professional leadership vision, is it black and white, dull, and non-descriptive? Or is it vivid, high-definition, and full of clarity? Embracing this shift and steering toward a clearer vision will result in greater courage, conviction, and confidence in your leadership and life. Dream big and don't let fear hold you back.

## COMMON CHARACTERISTICS

Consider these common characteristics of successful, visionary leaders:

| | | |
|---|---|---|
| Intelligence | Fearless | Creative |
| Life-long learner | Disciplined | Passionate |
| Focused forward | Growth Mindset | Risk-taker |
| Generous | Committed | Goal and Action-oriented |
| Highly Motivated | Influential | Grow From Mistakes |

# VISION FROM YOUR MIND'S EYE

**MIKE:** In college, I traveled to India to help host educational events at public schools. Public speaking was becoming a larger part of my life and I had the opportunity to speak to over a thousand attendees at one of our events. One night, while lying in bed and sweating profusely in the New Delhi heat, I let my mind wander...

I saw myself—in my mind's eye—backstage in a very large auditorium. I peeked through the curtain to see the layout of the stage, and surveyed the assembling audience. I took notice of the details: the feeling of the curtain separating the backstage from the front. I noticed the energy of the crowd. I saw myself walking out to meet a packed auditorium. That night, inspired by my success in India, I vividly saw myself stand with confidence and composure in front of thousands of people. Sitting up I wrote down my vision in my journal.

### VISION DIRECTS DECISIONS.

That mental picture stayed with me through college, training for nationals in collegiate debate, and my early career days. At times I misplaced that picture and other times I preoccupied myself with the pleasures of life: I married Taylor, we had our son, and I settled into a nice leadership position. However, even though this vision was displaced at times, it was never lost.

With that exact picture in mind, my wife and I made a dramatic move, upending our comfortable life in Washington for a very different life in California. Then it happened.

The courageous California move brought about dramatic changes, and along with it an invite to step out behind a black curtain, into the lights, onto the stage in front of thousands of people.

It is eerie to note how similar the mental picture I received in India matched to the reality in California. It is also very reassuring.

Crafting a clear mental picture of your eventual outcome directs your current decisions. Afterall, to get where you want to go, you have to first know where you want to go and where to start. Without clarity of vision, you won't know either.

To obtain a high-definition vision, begin to write down the specifics. Describe in detail what you will do. Determine what kind of leader you will be. Don't just repeat the status quo. Imagine a reality beyond what you can see right now.

## BEYOND WHAT YOU SEE RIGHT NOW

**STEVE:** I clearly remember sitting in Bob's Big Boy (my favorite restaurant) near Sunset Boulevard in Los Angeles, California. As a college senior, I relished my Saturday evening cheeseburger and fries basket followed by Bob's chocolate brownie. I would hit up Bob's at 10pm with two of my buddies every week to ponder our futures:

- *Where will we live and work?*

- *When would we get married?*

- *Would we make a significant contribution in our lifetimes that really mattered?*

- *What were our dreams? Our purpose?*

Looking back, the answers to our questions were simplistic. I remember saying, "I think there is more beyond what we can see right now." Right after I said that, I looked down the street and noticed a movie marquee a block away. I said, "Hey guys, what do you think is playing at that movie theater?" One of my friends quickly read the title out loud and then questioned, "Can't you see that, Steve?"

I couldn't.

I needed glasses! Within weeks, I had a new prescription. I discovered that I had been missing out on vision, and that there was much more beyond what I could literally see.

In life and leadership, this is often the case. There is more beyond what we can see right now.

## TIME FOR A NEW VISION

What if you took some quality time to stop and visualize a fresh new vision for your business?

Many leaders, paralyzed and fearful, find themselves stuck during dramatic shifts in the business world. We have to deal with the crises in this moment, but we also must not lose sight of what can be accomplished. Remind yourself of your vision.

*WHAT NEW OPPORTUNITIES DO YOU SEE IN THE MIDST OF*
*TURBULENT CHANGE?*
*HOW CAN YOU LEAD YOURSELF TOWARD RESETTING*
*A NEW VISION?*

What can you achieve in the next 3 months that matters most? And what's possible in the next 6 months that gains momentum? In a year's time?

## CASE STUDY: WES HERMAN

Wes Herman is the founder and CEO of Woods Coffee, a popular coffeehouse chain of nineteen locations based in the Pacific Northwest. Since its inception in 2002, the company has grown consistently in popularity and profitability.

Wes and his family relocated to Lynden, Washington from southern California. They purchased a large farm and focused on raising their four kids there while Wes recovered from a life-threatening illness. With Wes' background in the coffee industry, his wife suggested, "Why don't we start a coffee shop?"

Wes was inspired. "Why don't we teach the kids how to write a business plan?"

The family sat in the living room and envisioned possibilities. They dreamed, discussed, and debated. They laughed and worked. They created a business plan that would allow them to grow quickly, enough to open a second store in just six months after opening the first store. They wanted Woods Coffee to be taken seriously.

They envisioned a company that would expand to multiple stores and create wealth for future generations. They also defined their values: to serve others, make a difference, and have fun.

Woods Coffee launched with two stores in 2002.

## VISION INTERRUPTED BY FEAR

Then, Wes went to prison.

While planning Woods Coffee, Wes was accused of mail fraud by an insurance company. He'd been collecting payments while being physically unable to work after contracting encephalitis, a viral disease. After a lengthy legal battle, he agreed to a plea bargain of one count of mail fraud for sending a check across state lines.

While dealing with the authorities and lawyers, and transitioning into prison, Wes encountered true fear. He said, "I was afraid of how this type of thing would impact our business. I experienced fear of the unknown, of how this would play out. I was also afraid of going to prison. How would this affect my family? Those were the very real fears that I had."

The more Wes focused on the impending challenges, the greater the fear grew. When we focus on fear, vision begins to collapse.

Wes' very clear vision momentarily faded and became colorless as the darkness of fear threatened his dreams.

During this dark time, Wes leaned into his faith. He remembered how in the past, in 1992, he had lost everything and made a come-back. He remembered challenges he had overcome when he held onto his faith in God. He said, "I realized that when I focused on the adventure of it all, and the things I learned along the way, I was able to keep fear from controlling me."

## VISION CLARIFIED

Wes served his one-year sentence, and in the meantime, his team focused on the clarity of their vision. Prison was a time for Wes to further reflect and to hone his vision. Wes and his company endured the test.

He went on to offer this advice to others: "As a CEO, creating a vision is paramount for growth. It's equally important to have the right team to execute that vision. Once you have your team in place, it's your job to know how and when to share that clear vision for maximum results."

## DISCOVER PLUS ULTRA VISION

Before the Italian explorer, Christopher Columbus, set sail for Spain in 1492 and discovered the Americas, the Spaniards believed that their country was the last westward point of solid land on a flat earth. Spanish coins were inscribed in Latin, *"ne plus ultra"*, meaning "no more beyond."

Imagine how *"ne plus ultra"* can be engraved on our minds. Sometimes we create self-imposed boundaries, sometimes we live by hurtful messages from the people who are closest to us.

## MORE BEYOND

We need to remove the *"ne"* from *"plus ultra".*

**MIKE:** Our family move to California didn't turn out the way I had hoped. There were moments when depression threatened to bury my dreams. Thankfully, my friend Jason and my wife Taylor invited me to shift my vision. My once high-definition TV was broken, but that wasn't the only high-definition TV out there.

### *YOU CAN SHIFT TO A NEW VISION.*

I shifted, and I chose to dream again. A year later, I was speaking to new audiences, coaching new businesses, and I had published my first book. I even received a phone call and was offered the opportunity to work with Royalty!

When I shifted, I allowed room for a new vision, I was able to remove the "ne" and discover my "plus ultra" vision.

**STEVE:** There were two or three turning points in my career where I was invited to share my vision of leadership and emotional intelligence on stage with other leading experts and regarded authorities around the country. I wanted to inspire greatness in others, but sometimes I'd find myself affected by discouraging cautions from fearful people. Like Mike, I was hearing a lot of "ne plus ultra".

I stuck to my guns, and last year, I delivered a keynote on the same stage as my mentor, John Maxwell, and Hall of Famer, Magic Johnson, inspiring over 1,500 Pharmaceutical CEOs and leaders to *Unleash the Leader Inside Themselves.* Thankfully, I didn't listen to the small thinkers and naysayers.

## PLUS ULTRA VISION FOR *YOU*

*First:* Lock in your own personal belief that there is always more beyond. A plus ultra may be improving your marriage, getting in shape, or rebuilding your organization to be lean, mean, and more profitable.

*Second:* Heed the advice of Wes Herman, as well as other leaders you admire. Remember and rehearse inspiring quotes. Keep "plus ultra" people around you and in front of you.

# PLUS ULTRA VISION

*"Vision is a picture of the future which creates passion in the present."*—Steve Gutzler

*"It's not just what you see, but what you don't see that determines your destination."*—Mike Acker

*"Your time is limited, so don't waste it living someone else's life."*—Steve Jobs

*"When you have exhausted all possibilities, remember this: you haven't."*—Thomas A. Edison

*"Example is leadership."*—Albert Schweitzer

*"Formulate and stamp indelibly on your mind a mental picture of yourself succeeding. Hold this picture tenaciously. Never permit it to fade."*

—Norman Vincent Peale

*"You are never too old to set another goal or to dream a new dream."*—C.S. Lewis

*"Put good and uplifting thoughts in your mind, because our thoughts determine our destiny, and our destiny determines our legacy."*—Steve Gutzler

*"Where you are is not where you have to stay."*
—Mike Acker

*Third:* Take out a blank page and begin to clarify your current dream. Maybe it's time to throw away an old dream and focus on a new one, maybe dream bigger. Where will you be in 12-24 months, 3-5 years, and in your next decade? Write out the values you will embrace, what causes you will support, what networks you will join, what locations you will explore, and what obstacles you will overcome.

Fourth: Take a deep breath and take the next step. Taking a first step toward your clarified vision begins that 3° shift which leads to a whole new direction. Don't wait. Do it now.

## VISION FOR YOUR LEADERSHIP AND YOUR LIFE

**MIKE:** One of the brand CEOs I work with shared his incredibly detailed vision for his company. His vision is not just high-definition, it is 4k Ultra High-Definition! The results are outstanding. His global brand is extremely profitable and impactful.

His vision for his company, however, was overshadowing other visions he had for his life. The pressures of his career weighed on him personally.

As leaders, we don't live compartmentalized lives. The personal bleeds into the professional, and the professional bleeds into the personal.

I helped my client see these tendencies, and he was able to shift. He took time to map out what he wanted his personal life to look like. Vision is not just for what you *do*, it is for *you*.

**IN ADDITION TO THE BUSINESS, INC, YOU NEED TO CREATE A YOU INC.**

## Consider this variation of the Eight Rules for Life, from Richard Branson:

### 1. Just do it

- Believe it can be done
- Have goals
- Prepare well
- Help each other

### 2. Have fun

- Have fun and work hard, money will come
- Don't waste time, grab your chances
- Have a positive outlook on life
- When it's not fun, move on

### 3. Be bold

- Calculate the risks and take them
- Believe in yourself
- Chase your dreams and goals
- Have no regrets
- Keep your word

## 4. Challenge yourself

- Aim high

- Try new things

- Always try

## 5. Stand on your own two feet

- Rely on yourself

- Chase your dreams but live in the real world

- Work together

## 6. Live in the moment

- Live life and live it fully

- Enjoy every moment

- Reflect on your life

- Make every second count

- Don't have regrets

## 7. Value family and friends

- Put your family and team first

- Be loyal

- Face problems head on

- Pick the right people and reward talent

## 8. Have respect

- Be positive and respectful

- Do the right thing

- Keep your good name

- Be fair in all dealings

As you bring greater clarity to your company and leadership, take some time to clarify your personal values as well.

## RENEWING VISION WHEN VISION IS LOST

Our own successes grew from the trenches. We've both been at low, broken points.

**MIKE:** As I published my first book, I was at a huge crossroads. I had just made a massive career change without a backup plan. My wife and I stood in our living room discussing the details of our budget and wondering what would come up next. We passionately debated what to do and where to allocate our time, energy, and money. I had taken a leap without a parachute.

Taylor and I were staring fear directly in the face.

One week later, I expanded my coaching business with a key company, launched a communication program, and began to work with a Fortune 500 company. One week, we were threatened to give into fear; the next week, we discovered a whole new path ahead.

**STEVE:** My company, Steve Gutzler and Leadership Quest, was founded during four months of unemployment. Rock bottom was a great place to build a foundation. I couldn't see then that in the future I'd partner with iconic companies and global brands such as Microsoft, LinkedIn, Ritz Carlton, Seattle Seahawks, Spotify, the US Department of Commerce, and the FBI National Academy of Washington.

When I was unemployed, we had just $700 in the bank. A neighbor knocked on our door to say, "Steve, I heard you are looking for your next opportunity. I've experienced unemployment, and my wife and I would like to share a gift with you." He handed me an envelope and I opened it to see several hundred dollar bills inside.

Julie and I wept in our kitchen, amazed and thankful for this remarkable act of kindness. It gave us hope to keep on going. This was just enough to do exactly that—to keep going! It was just enough to believe that there was more beyond what we could see.

You might be reading this while living through your own difficult time. Uncertainty happens to all of us. I've learned that my well-designed "plan A" can and will dissolve, only to discover "plan B" is remarkable.

Before I was married, an older gentleman shared these five stages of marriage:

1. Romance

2. Reality

3. Resentments

4. Rebellion

5. Rebuilding and restoring

He reminded me that the 5th stage was the most important.

I believe that's not only true for marriage, but also for all areas of life and business. Get your vision focused on stage five: Rebuild and Restore.

Thomas Edison had his entire life's savings invested in his numerous experiments in a large warehouse, only to watch it catch fire and burn to the ground. He lost everything. He spent the entire night watching it burn and smolder. The next morning, his son found him sifting through the debris and rubble. His son was afraid his father's spirit would be absolutely crushed, but to his amazement, Edison looked up and said, "I've been thinking: we can retrieve a lot of this metal and debris to sell as scrap in order to rebuild. Let's get to work."

> *"Yesterday is gone. Tomorrow has not yet come. We only have today. Let us begin."*
>
> —Mother Teresa

## WOW LEADS TO HOW

Ritz Carlton Hotel expects all employees to do whatever it takes to make the guest's experience so memorable and so satisfying that they will not only come back, but they will also tell others about their experience. This is the goal of the Ritz Carlton's "guest satisfaction above all" culture.

To maintain this culture and keep the vision high-definition, the Ritz Carlton employees tell stories. They tell the Ritz Carlton "wow stories."

Every Monday and Friday, every week, in every Ritz Carlton hotel around the world, employees gather to share "wow stories". Simon Cooper, former President of Ritz Carlton, says, "Wow stories are about the great things our ladies and gentlemen have done." These stories recognize people who stand out, and they inspire employees to create service behaviors that bring customers back again and again.

A waiter at the Ritz Carlton in Dubai overheard a conversation between a gentleman and his wife at dinner. The husband was saying that it was a shame he could not take his wife, who was in a wheelchair, to the beach for a sunset dinner. The waiter shared this with his co-workers, including the food and beverage manager. Everybody worked together. The next evening, waitstaff assisted the woman along a wooden walkway leading down to the beach where a candlelit dinner for two was enjoyed in a private tent.

How many guests do you think that couple have steered to the Ritz Carlton?

As you clarify your vision, allow the WOW to lead to HOW, and you will do what you plan to do.

# SHIFT

How can you achieve your own high-definition vision? Look inward.

Life is too short to leave your best on the shelf. Get clear! What are your "must have outcomes"? Are they realistic and doable?

1.  What do you aspire to do? In the next 12-14 months, in 3-5 years, and in the next decade?

2.  What are the emotionally compelling reasons that will drive you? What are the benefits to you and to others? What is the lasting legacy?

3.  Who will help you achieve your goals? Do you need guidance from experts? Do you need the support of a coach or mentor?

4.  Is your vision in alignment with your passions, your values, and a juicy part of your life's story?

Think about the person you want to become as a leader.

1.  Why do you strive to lead? What's most important to you as a leader? What's a complete waste of time?

2.  What kind of leader do you want to be? What leadership qualities are important to you?

3.  What is your personal development plan? Who is in your inner circle and strengthens you? What are you saying "no" to in order to say "yes" to your best?

4.  What positive habits must you stay disciplined in? What keeps you balanced and sane? What brings you child-like joy and deep satisfaction?

*DON'T LET COMPARISON KILL YOUR VISION.*
*DON'T LET SMALL THINKING KILL YOUR VISION.*
*DON'T LET THE PAST KILL YOUR VISION.*

*Insecure leaders never develop leaders, they replace them.*

—John C. Maxwell


*The more you know yourself, the more patience you have for what you see in others.*

—Erik Erikson

## FOURTH SHIFT:
# FROM INSECURE TO CONFIDENT

Have you ever worked with an insecure leader?

As you read that question, you may have nodded or smiled sadly. There are numerous ways insecurity shows up in leadership. Consider these common caricatures:

## PORTRAITS OF INSECURITY

### THE POWER TRIPPER

This leader shows up and demands respect, loyalty, and obedience. They desire to be seen as the boss and the one in charge. Each command carries an implicit "or else". This type of leader climbed through the ranks, paid their dues, and now gives orders to others who are on the lower rungs of the ladder.

### THE AVOIDER

Some insecure people rise to leadership but lack the ability to make tough decisions. Second-guessing becomes third-guessing, fourth-guessing, and so on. As decisions become more and more difficult, the avoider becomes hard to find, buried in spreadsheets, or walled up in their private office. They hope that if they don't make a decision now, then the problem might just go away. They don't realize or care that tension mounts each moment a decision is avoided.

## THE ATTENTION HOARDER

Larger than life, this character is all charisma and charm. Personality is the chief reason this person rose to leadership heights. People want to be noticed by this leader, because it makes them feel special. However, the Attention Hoarder is so focused on being liked and noticed, that it leaves little room for anyone else. This person lives for the spotlight and constantly speaks in "I" and "me" language.

## THE BLAMER

This kind of leader acutely realizes the mistakes of the organization and its people and is constantly pointing it out. They want each person to understand the "reality" of their faults, while being completely ignorant of their own.

## THE MICROMANAGER

Perhaps the most common of insecure leaders, the Micromanager worries that no one will do the job quite as well as they do. They *have* to stay close to those they oversee in order to make sure that others know how to do it the only right way: *their* way. The Micromanager tends to work more than anyone else because, after all, if all of the jobs are going to be done right, it has to be done by them.

## THE DISTANT DELEGATOR

Opposite to the Micromanager is the Distant Delegator. This individual figures that their people know how to do their job, and so they give out tasks and get out of the way. *Way* out of the way. Often, they imagine that others know how to do most things better than they do, so they keep offloading jobs. They don't always ensure that these people have the capacity or the qualifications to accomplish the tasks. This type of leader dumps duties on others and then disappears.

## THE COMPLIMENT FISHER

Compliment Fishers are people who regularly need compliments to assure themselves that they are doing well. Instead of being confident in their own abilities and accomplishments, they seek external sources to praise their work and actions. For this to be an insecurity, it needs to go beyond the common desire to be recognized; instead, the insecure person turns every action into an action that needs to be appreciated.

As you read these caricatures, you probably recalled a leader that made your life difficult. Even if you liked that teacher, manager, or CEO, you never felt sure of your ability to perform. Insecure leaders create insecurity in those who follow.

**MIKE:** I once worked for someone who struggled with self-doubt. I was fairly confident, but over time, I noticed that I began to doubt myself. It was infectious!

### INSECURE LEADERS CREATE INSECURE CULTURES.

Unfortunately, we can relate as we have seen insecurity show up in our own leadership, "Hey, Matt, what did you think about the speech? Did you feel like people were into it?" Coming off the stage, I probed my teammate for positive feedback. I knew the talk went well, but because of my insecurity, I wanted to hear it from someone else.

**STEVE:** "Honey, did you realize I cleaned the kitchen? Pretty good." I have asked this question to my wife on numerous occasions. My wife sees through my fishing excursion. She gives me the same wry smile, responding, "Yes, I do that every night."

While fishing for compliments is an easy out for telling on ourselves, we have also power-tripped, avoided, hoarded attention, blamed, micromanaged, and delegated. We are not beyond insecure leadership, and neither are you.

Embrace the shift from a previous chapter and become self-aware. Stay conscious of how your insecurity affects your leadership, which is an indirect way of saying: your insecurity affects your people.

# THE ORIGIN OF INSECURITY

*INSECURE LEADERS OPERATE FROM FEAR.*

Carin managed a nationally recognized retail corporate franchise. Her location won national awards, earned millions each year, and employed a large team. She was (and is) extremely successful.

She had worked her way up through the ranks. She exuded what it means to work hard. She also worked long. Too long. As a result, her management team worked hard, and they worked long. When team members cut back to mere fifty or sixty hour work weeks, they feared the stare they knew they would receive. While Carin was well-loved, she was also resented. Hourly employees avoided entering management because they knew Carin silently expected her team to work sixty to eighty hours, just like she did.

Unlike the other top managers of her company, Carin did not have a college degree. She feared that she would get passed up for promotion, and that she was looked down upon by her own team. Carin's fear drove her into work addiction. Her insecurity affected her team, family, and future.

# HOW FEAR SHOWS UP

*REMEMBER: INSECURE LEADERS OPERATE FROM FEAR.*

Fear shows up in many different forms:

- Fear of falling behind their peers
- Fear of missing out on opportunities
- Fear of making bad decisions
- Fear of not being recognized
- Fear of being found out as an imposter
- Fear of not realizing goals
- Fear of not living up to standards
- Fear of failing

To shift toward confidence, take a moment to identify your fears.

Insecurity is often easy to spot in others, but easy to miss in ourselves. To make the shift away from fear-based leadership, you must *recognize* where and to what extent insecurity hides inside of you.

You might not totally resemble one of the insecure caricatures at the beginning of the chapter, but any and all insecurities you feel are transmitted to the team you lead. When the leader is insecure, the team cannot fully realize their potential.

## WORKING WITH A LEADER WHO OPERATES IN FEAR

Here are ten questions designed to identify your insecurities:

1. Do you feel threatened by the skills of others?

2. Do you avoid difficult conversations?

3. Do you feel the need to give explanations for setbacks?

4. Do you gloss over negative feedback?

5. Do you feel like you already know the answers instead of forming questions?

6. Do you feel the need to take credit?

7. Do you micromanage your team?

8. Do you begrudgingly celebrate the success of others?

9. Do you get mad at others, only to realize it wasn't really worth the anger?

10. Do you constantly compare yourself to other leaders?

# CASE STUDY: JERRY LEISURE

Jerry Leisure is the CEO and Co-Founder of Officium Labs, where a customer experience marketplace is designed to help improve people's lives through entertainment and customer service. Through Jerry's leadership, they are transforming the gaming and entertainment customer experiences. He stands and walks with confidence; you can't miss his 6'4" frame.

Jerry struggled to find a management position early on in his career because he lacked mentorship as a leader. He was finally hired into a management position at Monster.com. Soon after his hiring, his confidence took a big hit. Although he was strategically a high performer, Jerry's leadership skills were scoring pretty low. He needed to work on his emotional intelligence.

And so Jerry did something courageous. He took a significant step back in his career progression in order to step forward as a leader. He decided to take a demotion to seek out a boss and mentor who could coach him on leadership.

He identified four critical areas of improvement:

- How leaders develop confidence

- How leaders treat people

- How leaders inspire

- How leaders engage peers and colleagues to be life-long learners

Jerry worked with his mentor and coach. Eventaully he shifted into a position at Microsoft. He went on to a leadership position in the gaming industry. He gained more clarity and built up his leadership confidence. He's currently the CEO of Officium Labs.

Jerry now asks these questions of himself:

1. Who am I as a person and as a leader?

2. How can I help our team find purpose and meaning in their work?

3. How can I live by and display our values daily?

4. How can I inspire greatness and confidence in others?

Confidence is like the stock market. There are highs and lows, and if we don't sell ourselves short, we'll always come back strong. For Jerry, leadership has been a journey, not a destination.

Confidence in leadership is a must. You can't fake it. Authentic confidence comes with focused effort. And when the leader grows, the team grows.

## CONFIDENCE IS A MASTERY SKILL

To shift from insecure to confident, understand that it's a mastery skill. You may want to begin with some of the same steps Jerry took:

- Listen more, speak less

- Engage with others without interrupting them

- Strive to be more collaborative

- Communicate clearly and stick to the message

- Eliminate annoying behaviors and distracting habits

- Be calm and confident under stress rather than becoming reactive

## REAL CONFIDENCE MAKES A REAL DIFFERENCE

**MIKE:** When I reflect on my early leadership assignments, I fondly remember Tony Cloud, an excellent entrepreneur, executive, and speaker. I began working for him in 2003. He quickly took me under his wing, making sure I felt supported and utilized. Four years later, Tony resigned and suggested that I take on his position.

Under my leadership, our organization advanced rapidly. When I later connected with Tony, I hesitated to share my success. I didn't want him to think that I thought I was better than him.

But he wouldn't let me hide. He asked detailed questions, and after learning about my successes, he smiled and joked, "Mike! That's incredible! I should have left a long time ago!"

In retrospect, I see that my early success was built on the groundwork Tony laid out for me. Due to his personal confidence, he selflessly encouraged and supported his staff. An insecure leader would have needed the credit, thinking they'd done the hard work previously. Tony allowed me to enjoy my moment. And he enjoyed it too, knowing he was part of my story.

President Truman has this to say about leaders who empower their teams and allow others to celebrate their success:

> *"It is amazing what you can accomplish if you do not care who gets the credit."*
>
> —Harry S. Truman

## GREAT WORK AWAITS YOU

As you shift away from insecurity and toward confidence, you will be able to do greater work than you have ever done. Some of that work won't carry your name, but they will silently be a part of your legacy. Some of that work won't even personally involve you; the work will be done by the people you lead. You will do more not by doing more, but by raising up more people.

*GREAT WORK IS PERFORMED WITH STRENGTH AND COURAGE, NOT FEAR AND INSECURITY.*

## THE TRIAD EXAMPLE

Co-founder of Market Impact, Dan Albaum, does transformational work with people and partners with B2B technology companies in order to elevate their brands. When Dan confronts uncertainty he employs his "Leadership Triad", which is Empowerment, Transparency, and Accountability. When he feels his team is out of alignment, he calls upon this system:

- How can I empower my team and keep the priority on a servant leadership mindset?

- Am I transparent in all communication—the good news and the not-so-good news?

- Are we mutually accountable for our performance and results?

He said, "I've discovered if I keep my triad front and center, I lead with confidence, not insecurity."


## THE GOAL OF CONFIDENCE

Confidence is not about us.

Confidence is not about impressing. It's about influencing.

Confidence is misguided if it stems from personal charisma, attention, and getting to the top. Confidence is about getting *others* to the top. Standing on top of the world by yourself, after all, is a very lonely place to be. Any big gust of wind up there can knock you down.

The "top" in the NFL is the Hall of Fame, the MVP, the teams playing Pro-Bowl, the first round pick, and, of course, the Super Bowl Champions.

Another coveted 'top' comes from the Electronics Arts (EA) video game series "Madden." Every year, a new player becomes the titular character of the game. Players count it as an honor to be selected by fans and by EA Games.

For the release of Madden 15, EA announced that Seahawks player Richard Sherman had won, beating famed Carolina Panthers quarterback, Cam Newton. Most players would be thrilled to receive the honor, but Sherman knew that no player arrived at any top on their own. He lobbied to have Earl Thomas, Kam Chancellor, and Byron Maxwell join him, knowing that together they had created the strong defense for which he himself was being recognized.

In the end, EA still decided to feature Sherman on his own. However, for the first time, they replaced their regular welcome screen to include all four players!

Sherman displayed true confidence. He didn't hoard all of the attention. He worked to share the accolades with his contributing teammates.

> *"The measure of a leader is not the number of people who serve him but the number of people he serves."*
>
> —John C. Maxwell

**STEVE:** One of my favorite clients is the president of a company of a leading national household brand. One thing you'll notice about him almost immediately is his personal confidence. He walks and speaks confidently, and he is an active listener. He remembers details for when he sees you again and asks insightful follow-up questions. His team and his customers are drawn to him.

Recently, I visited him at his corporate office. His executive assistant met me in the lobby and greeted me warmly, as usual. After our meeting, this very busy and in-demand leader walked me back down to the lobby, a gracious act. He connected with three or four people on our return to the lobby, offering praise along the way. What impressed me most was how "in the moment" he was with his team members. There is no doubt he possesses the confidence to lift up others and he shines while praising others on his team.

Meanwhile, insecure and fearful leaders exclude others. They miss these golden moments of connection.

True confidence and connection always begin with a commitment to someone else.

A reporter once asked the Hall-of-Famer baseball player Joe DiMaggio, "Joe, you always seem to play ball with the same confidence and intensity. You run out every grounder and race after every fly ball, even in the dog days of August when the Yankees have a big lead in the pennant race and there's nothing on the line. How do you do it?"

DiMaggio replied, "I always remind myself that there will be someone in the stands who's never seen me play before." While DiMaggio certainly gained personal satisfaction in his performance, he indicated that he constantly worked hard to honor his audience.

That kind of others-oriented mindset is what a leader must maintain in order to lead with authentic confidence.

## CREATE YOUR 3D HABITS (DISCIPLINE, DRIVE, AND DETERMINATION)

Habits are the micro-actions we perform, in between the big actions that drive big results. The best approach isn't to simply eliminate unwanted behaviors but to *replace* them with new habits.

### HERE ARE THREE HABITS TO SHIFT TOWARD OVER THE NEXT 90 DAYS:

### 1. START WITH DISCIPLINE

In the show 'Survivor', contestants must learn how to survive and thrive to win the reality TV show contest. Contestants immediately search for water, food, and shelter. However, fire becomes the first requirement in order to survive, since it is used to sanitize the water source and provide warmth at night and for cooking. Those contestants who prioritize the discovery of their fire source are always the most successful.

In leadership, we too must discover our *fire source* to survive and thrive. For the leader, the fire source is personal, daily disciplines.

Discipline is the daily spark in our leadership that ignites the fire of our habits. Those fires must be lit daily, and discipline provides the first step of energy.

Examples of Daily Discipline Habits:

- Set a consistent sleep and rise time.

- Make your bed in the morning. According to Navy Seal Admiral, William H. McRaven, "If you want to change the world, start by making your bed in the morning."

- Schedule your daily workout, even if it's just 20 minutes. Small 3° shifts, compounded over time, create extraordinary results.


## 2. PERSONAL DRIVE

**STEVE:** My son, Jayce, served over five years as a Special Weapons and Tactics Team (SWAT) Officer. Becoming a SWAT officer was a long-time career aspiration of his. Jayce's personal drive was key. He trained and prepared to pass various tests in order to fulfill the tactical standards and skills necessary to be SWAT-worthy.

What are your aspirations right now? You'll need confidence in yourself and your abilities. Think of yourself as a corporate athlete or an elite performer. Write out your career aspirations.

What will you need to prepare for in order to reach these goals?

What skills will you need to develop?

### 3. GRIT AND DETERMINATION

**MIKE:** As we set out to write this book, my schedule was very full and family obligations were significant with a toddler in the house. I was determined, though, and set a strict schedule to write. I wrote early in the mornings, sometimes before 5 am. I wrote late in the evenings, long after my family went to sleep.

High performers aren't always naturally talented. They are likely the hardest workers. Determine to go forward every day.

*"Success seems to be largely a matter of hanging on after others have let go."*

—William Feather

## SHIFT WITH A 90-DAY CONFIDENCE CHALLENGE

What are you preparing for right now? Are you working on a big presentation? Are you creating a game-changing proposal? Are you leading a team offsite for the first time? Are you working on a speech? Are you interviewing for your next career move?

For the next 90 days, harness confidence and push through your quitting points.

Find courage to take on any limiting belief, or behavior, that has been holding you back.

To make the shift away from fear and toward confident leadership, consider some of these actions:

- Create the game plan. What small steps will you take daily? Small 3° shifts create compounding momentum

- Write down and denounce limiting behaviors that hold you back

- Define your personal convictions

- Walk taller and smile more often. Body language produces stronger self-confidence

- Focus on positive emotions. Remember, positive emotions drive positive results

These actions will help you attack fear with a new energy of innate confidence.

*Some things are not necessarily wrong; they're just not necessary.*

—Rick Warren

*Each day we choose to live the legacy we want to leave.*

—Pam Farrel

# FIFTH SHIFT:
# FROM ACTIVITY TO ACCOMPLISHMENT

There is a sense of deep satisfaction when you check off completed tasks on your to-do list. That's why most leaders we coach and the teams we work with are addicted to their to-do lists. Busy activities dominate their days. And that's the key word: *activities*.

## WHAT IS IMPORTANT

In 2019, Susanne became the Director of Leadership and Talent Development for a large medical supplier. Susanne is a very thorough and detail-oriented leader. She even creates systems for creating systems. This organizational prowess led to incredible personal success. And then her corporate systems led to companywide success, which brought about increased recognition. As a result, she achieved an early directorial promotion.

In this manner, Susanne kept gaining momentum until she was abruptly confronted by the reality that the new hiring process she implemented for her company was very poorly received.

**MIKE:** When I began working with her, she asked, "Where did I go wrong with our onboarding system?"

"Help me understand what you do, Susanne," I said.

She first relayed her professional history, and then described her current position. Once I grasped her background, she outlined her process for reinventing the new hiring process and the onboarding presentation. Since Susanne is incredibly detailed, I felt like I had a thorough grasp on the situation.

After I understood the context, Susanne cued up her presentation. I clicked on my timer, and forty-five minutes later, I understood what had happened.

While Susanne's *delivery* displayed professionalism, humor, and leadership, her teaching was overloaded. Her content contained every single possible item a new employee could find useful.

In 45 minutes, she had covered over 50 points of information.

*IF EVERYTHING IS IMPORTANT, NOTHING IS.*

## WHAT DO YOU WANT PEOPLE TO KNOW?

Not knowing how much longer the speech would last, I raised my hand. She paused and smiled. "What did I do wrong?"

"Susanne, what do you want people to know?" I asked.

She was confused, and she went back through her slides. "Umm. Is it not clear? Did I miss something?"

"Not at all. You told me everything, and you still had more to say. I'm overwhelmed with content. There's no way I can remember everything."

As we worked together, Susanne adjusted her messaging. Her willingness to make cuts along with intentional focus helped her create a wildly successful program. One sentence stood out to her in this process, and it should stand out to you too:

*IF YOU TRY TO SAY EVERYTHING, YOU SAY NOTHING.*

Her initial trainees were overwhelmed because they struggled to identify what they were supposed to remember, prioritize, and act upon. Her subsequent presentations contained far less content, and made greater impact. She made the shift from saying everything to making sure she said the most important parts.

She learned a variation of the classic principle: quality over quantity. This is what the fifth shift is about: Activity (though it often feels good) can block true accomplishment.

## MOST VALUABLE & PROFITABLE (MVPs)

One of the most significant shifts a leader can make is from activity-based days to accomplishment-based days. It's important to clarify the MVP tasks.

**STEVE:** Brian Jeide, one of my best friends and trusted advisors, challenged me to a "time audit." I'd had one of the busiest, and most frustrating, years of my life. The audit was a courageous (and sometimes painful) investigation, and we discovered that only 10% to 15% of my days were focused on MVP work. I was so addicted to the feeling of conquering my to-do lists that I'd lost sight of the *important* work that really led to performance and profits!

I'll never forget the advice Brian offered: "Steve, if you can increase the time you spend doing MVP work from 10-15% to 25-30%, you can double your influence and income."

Fourteen months later, that's exactly what happened.

*SHIFT FROM LOW-VALUE ACTIVITIES TO ACCOMPLISHMENTS.*

## GRATIFICATION AND FRUSTRATION

Short-term gratification, like crossing off 20 things on your to-do list, doesn't mean you get important MVP work done.

Shorter lists are simply more effective. Checklists are an opportunity to identify the important priorities. Law enforcement professionals have very important checklists of basic protocols. They create short lists of three to eight *priority projects*.

Leaders who get inundated with too many tasks get little finished, or little finished *well*. It leads to frustration, exhaustion, and lack of profitability. Initially, checking off long lists might feel gratifying, but in the end, it is futile. The bottom line is that working on the wrong things is a waste of time and energy.

Make the 3° shift toward accomplishment.

Steve Jobs, former CEO of Apple, only worked on six to eight projects at a time. He was a master delegator, outsourcing low-value tasks. His focus was on high-value initiatives: the Mac, the launch of the latest iPhone and iPad, opening new Apple stores, and the launch of iTunes to transform the music industry. Jobs was successful because he was *selective*.

When you look at your to-do list, how many items are game-changers? What is producing growth and sustainable profits? Smart leaders are only working on three to eight priority projects.

## CASE STUDY: MELISSA AGNES

Melissa Agnes is the founder and CEO of Crisis Ready Institute. She is recognized as a leading authority on crisis preparedness, reputation management, and brand protection. She is also the creator of the Crisis Ready™ Model and the author of *Crisis Ready: Building an Invincible Brand in an Uncertain World*. She's a popular speaker, and an advisor to some of today's leading organizations facing the greatest risks.

Melissa draws upon her remarkable experience in helping global brands and world leaders prevent and overcome a range of real-world, high-impact crises. She's an outstanding leader who is passionate about reminding us that daily activities do not need to drive all our days; we must think short *and* long term, even in the midst of worldwide crises.

## THINK LONG TERM AND FOCUS ON EMOTIONAL CONNECTION

During our interview with Melissa, she explained that right now, the world (i.e., your customers, employees, community, etc.) is trying to survive. She challenges, "Does your creative strategy bring something of value to them at this time?" This value can be in the form of support (whether emotional, physical, or financial), hope, reassurance, leadership, or peace of mind for a given moment.

While part of your Crisis Ready™ strategy and tactics are to survive (especially in times like these), it is important that you do not lose sight of the long game. The COVID-19 pandemic will eventually be behind us. Make no mistake: during uncertain times, your current circumstances will come to an end and you will survive this.

What is the emotional connection you want to have built with those you serve? That emotional connection should be part of your Crisis Ready™ long-term strategy. Focus on the accomplishment of connecting on a human level such that you care about customers and their team first.

Every true accomplishment that should guide your decisions as leaders needs to be filtered through the lens of others—their needs, wants, and desires.

*ADD VALUABLE SERVICES, NOT JUST SERVICES.*

# DECLUTTER YOUR TO-DO LIST

According to USA Today, Clint Rovinescu was named CEO of Air Canada. When he took over the helm in 2009, the company was on the verge of bankruptcy. Thirteen months later, Air Canada was named the number-one airline in North America, flying to 175 destinations, with over 76,000 employees, and boasting 33 million customers per year.

Although he walked into a challenging, complex, and desperate crisis, Rovinescu had only four items on his to-do list.

He said, "Four priorities doesn't sound like a lot, but I want the entire organization – every person on staff – to focus on just these four things." This was an enormous shift.

As per the USA Today article, Rovinescu's MVP list included:

1.  Take $500 million in costs out of the company without cutting employee wages or benefits

2.  Re-engage the customer

3.  Elevate the Air Canada brand in international markets

4.  Change the culture from a government-owned mentality to a nimbler entrepreneur company

## COURAGE TO SHIFT

It takes courage to select the just three to eight projects, to shift from activity to accomplishment. Each project must be essential to growing the business, and it must be focused on the central vision, the *purpose* of the organization.

**STEVE:** When Brian Jeide challenged me to do the Time Audit, I made the shift to a short list:

- Cultivating strength

- Letting go of the instant gratification of checking off small items

- Demanding aggressive accountability from team members

- Daily prioritization around high-value MVP clients, work, and projects

It was tough to let go of that gratifying list of small tasks. I had to face the fear of missing out (FOMO). When we focus on saying and doing what is truly important, we inevitably neglect many problems we can immediately solve. For me, it triggered the feeling that something was missing, that I was forgetting something.

FOMO shows up constantly in our professional lives. Drivers, go-getters, and achievers want to make sure everything gets done. In order to shift, you must realize that busy-ness doesn't lead to the accomplishment you desire.

Keep the list short. Shift from being busy to being productive.

# ANOTHER CONFESSION

**MIKE:** As I write this chapter with Steve, I realize I'm guilty of disobeying this rule! There is something I'm currently holding onto that I know I need to let go of. I've known this for a while. There is something I need to *stop*.

I've *prided* myself on accomplishing many of my goals and pursuing my dreams. I start almost every day by planning my actions and prioritizing my targets with the *SELF Journal* (https://bestself.co). This tool has helped me drop unneeded actions in exchange for what produces the most results. With felt-success I've had *pride* that I could do it all. As a result, I have held onto the role of president of the board of GO (goonthemission.com).

## *HOLDING ON TOO LONG HOLDS US BACK.*

Fear of letting go, fear of missing out, and fear of losing prestige keeps me occupied with e-mails, administrative duties, and commitments that could easily be transferred to someone else. This prevents GO from having a more available and focused leadership.

## *HOLDING ON TOO LONG HOLDS OTHERS BACK.*

So, while working on this book, I made the shift. I let go of my role. I am trusting that letting go will lead to greater things.

What about you? Where can you shift? What can you let go of? What do you need to stop?

# FROM START TO STOP LIST

We love conferences. In previous roles we have loved bringing our teams to conferences and currently we love speaking at conferences. At conferences, expectations are raised, cultures are examined, and new ideas are born. As much as we love conferences, we have one complaint: people overcommit.

Consider the last conference you attended. You probably listened to several speakers, attended a workshop or two, and visited a bunch of booths. By the end of a conference, minds are overflowing with ideas.

Many leaders return from conferences feeling motivated and inspired, and they initiate new systems and announce new tactics and strategies. Their teams begin to dread when their leaders go to a conference because they know another set of dramatic changes are on the way.

Inspiration is not a bad thing. It is just often insufficient.

In a recent workshop, a CEO started his session by asking, "What do you need to do?"

The room was full of ambitious entrepreneurs, and they immediately began taking notes. The speaker waited for a minute, watching the participants. Then he said, "If you wrote down something you need to start doing, cross it out." Everyone was confused.

"When I said, 'what do you need to do?' each of you thought that you needed to begin a new activity. Doing doesn't have to be starting something, it can also be stopping something. So, now, I want you to write down something you will commit to stopping."

On March 13, 2020, Bill Gates posted to his LinkedIn page:

> *I have made the decision to step down from both of the public boards on which I serve—Microsoft and Berkshire Hathaway—to dedicate more time to philanthropic priorities including global health and development, education, and my increasing engagement in tackling climate change. The leadership at the Berkshire companies and Microsoft has never been stronger, so the time is right to take this step.*

Bill Gates decided to eliminate two large commitments in order to focus his efforts on charitable priorities and to start new initiatives in the Gates Foundation. Bill understood that to accomplish his philanthropic MVPs, he needed to reduce activity elsewhere.

As you go through these next 90 days, follow the words of the CEO leading the workshop and the example of Bill Gates. Consider not what you can start, but what you can stop.

To accelerate in a manual car, you let go of the gas so that you can engage the clutch and shift up. If you never let go of the gas pedal, however, you will never go further or faster.

Over the next three months, for every new action you start, commit to stopping something else. What do you need to let go of?

# THE POWER OF NO

Staying focused on high-value projects requires a new level of tenacity. It takes self-discipline to say "No".

- Be conscious when deciding how you spend your time

- Avoiding the seduction of drifting away from your focus

- Ask yourself: What am I doing right now that will help me advance?

Make 'NO' the new normal. This will take practice, but remember, in order to rise up, you must clear away the clutter.

*IN ORDER TO GO UP, YOU MUST CLEAN UP. ACCEPT CHG*

**MIKE:** Marc Pearson led a large organization, served on boards, and restructured a non-profit that runs humanitarian efforts throughout the Pacific Northwest. I informally interned under Marc while I was in college. As I shadowed him, I noted that he was amazing at saying "NO". He was always gracious, but firm. Marc said "NO" to prestigious job offers, political possibilities, the speaking circuit, book deals, and to networking opportunities with prominent people. I clearly remember a very prestigious person asking him out to lunch. Marc smiled, then kindly and firmly said, "No, thanks."

I didn't understand it at the time. Marc said no to incredible opportunities. None of these options were inherently bad. On the contrary, many were very desirable and could have been very beneficial. However, he was not interested in building a resume; he was interested in leaving behind a legacy. Marc had clearly identified his MVPs.

Unfortunately, Marc's life was cut short as ALS (Lou Gehrig's disease) worked its way through his body.

Shortly before the disease claimed his life, he was wheeled onstage in front of over a thousand colleagues. Unable to move his hand, his wife received the LifeTime Achievement award bestowed on him by those who had been impacted by his leadership. Marc had earned this award at the age of 60.

*THINK MORE OF YOUR LEGACY THAN YOUR RESUME.*

In order to know what to stop, you must first determine the MVPs of your work and life. When you get these in place, you'll know what to eliminate.

## ROCK, PEBBLES, AND SAND

Over the last decade, the story of "The Rock, Pebbles, and Sand" swept across the internet and is often quoted in blogs, books, speeches, and movies. Its origins remain unknown.

*A philosophy professor stood before his class with some items on the table in front of him. When the class began, he wordlessly picked up a very large and empty mayonnaise jar and proceeded to fill it with rocks, about 2 inches in diameter.*

He then asked the students if the jar was full. They agreed that it was.

So the professor then picked up a box of pebbles and poured them into the jar. He shook the jar lightly. The pebbles, of course, rolled into the open areas between the rocks.

He then asked the students again if the jar was full. They agreed it was.

The professor picked up a box of sand and poured it into the jar. Of course, the sand filled up everything else.

He then asked once more if the jar was full. The students responded with a unanimous "Yes."

"Now," said the professor, "I want you to recognize that this jar represents your life. The rocks are the important things – your family, your partner, your health, your children – things that if everything else was lost and only they remained, your life would still be full.

The pebbles are the other things that matter – like your job, your house, your car.

The sand is everything else. The small stuff."

"If you put the sand into the jar first," he continued, "there is no room for the pebbles or the rocks. The same goes for your life.

If you spend all your time and energy on the small stuff, you will never have room for the things that are important to you. Pay attention to the things that are critical to your happiness. Play with your children. Take your partner out dancing. There will *always be time to go to work, clean the house, give a dinner party and fix the disposal.*

*Take care of the rocks first — the things that really matter. Set your priorities. The rest is just sand."*

Shift from activity to accomplishment by choosing the order in which you work on your priorities.

**PUT THE ROCKS IN FIRST.**

# THREE AREAS TO EXAMINE AND RESET

## 1. SELF-LEADERSHIP

The biggest daily battle of leadership is leading ourselves. We distract ourselves constantly.

*Will I have the extra cup of coffee?*
*Should I jump on email?*
*Do I feel up to working out or should I pass?*
*What's happening on Facebook?*
*Will I shut down early and regroup tomorrow?*

## FOCUS ON THE BENEFITS

When those temptations enter your mind, take five minutes to give yourself a quick mental pep talk. Remind yourself of your goals *and* the compelling reasons you want them. You are worth it. Remember what the old gospel preacher said, "God doesn't make no junk." You are a unique masterpiece focusing your energies.

Lead yourself. Push on physically, because you are worth it! Push on emotionally by managing your negative emotions. Push on each time with a new, creative, and innovative mindset.

## 2. LEAD OTHERS

Sometimes, the people you love and respect can be an interruption to your focus. Sometimes, they'll distract you for a quick chat. People won't value your time until you value it yourself. You may need to close your door for part of the day to get the MVP work done. If you work from home, select two or three working hours to be left alone to fully concentrate on your next big project.

You must choose to lead others by communicating your boundaries *clearly,* instead of letting others set the boundaries for you. Communicate:

- Your availability

- Your expectations

- Your priorities

## 3. LEAVE YOUR DEVICE

Today's leaders are held captive to technology. Smartphones give us immediate access to emails, and the constant onslaught of information. The average smartphone user checks their device every five to six minutes, that's an average of 150-160 times per day! Screen time averages 7-8 hours per day.

Don't be that device-addict who constantly checks their phone every 5 minutes. Switching tasks dilutes effectiveness. Isn't it amazing how a smartphone causes us to be so dumb?

**MIKE:** Steve and I have challenged each other to turn off our devices twice a day, to focus on the MVPs. No email, no voicemail, no texting, and no notifications for 90-minutes. This gives us a focused time block to get things done.

**STEVE:** One of my biggest breakthroughs was simply to charge my phone upstairs after 8:00pm every evening in order to be more present with my wife, Julie. Getting rid of the devices has work advantages as well as lifestyle advantages. Retrain your brain to focus on the most important items.

## SHIFT

To Increase Influence, Impact, and Income:

1. List ALL of your activities at work. You might include: Zoom calls, phone appointments, staff meetings, email management, projects, face-to-face meetings with

clients, sales calls, follow-up procedures, administrative work, expense reports, and scheduling.

2. Identify three things you do exceptionally well in your work.

3. Identify the top three MVP activities for your business.

4. Identify the three most important activities that you *don't like to do.*

5. Identify two low-value activities that are easy to delegate or outsource.

6. What is one thing you are doing right now that you should eliminate? What are the immediate benefits that will result from this decision?

In order to shift from activity to accomplishments, determine how you are wasting your valuable time and how you will create more time for your MVPs, and for the things that will result in the life you desire.

**WHERE YOU INVEST YOUR TIME DEFINES WHO YOU ARE.**

*The most powerful leadership tool you have
is your own personal example.*

—John Wooden


*It is health
that is real wealth
And not pieces
of gold and silver.*

—Mahatma Gandhi

# SIXTH SHIFT:
# FROM SMART TO SMART AND HEALTHY

**STEVE:** My family and I were enjoying a beautiful dinner at the iconic Mama's Fish House at the end of our vacation in Maui. We were sitting in the open-air dining area, sipping tropical drinks with little colorful umbrellas. We had enjoyed an amazing dinner: mahi mahi with macadamia nut cream sauce, swordfish, and fresh cod. I thought about how grateful I was for this tropical vacation with my wife Julie, our daughter Jenna, and our two sons, Jayce and Kyle.

In many respects, it was a milestone of a vacation together based on a lot of hard work, sometimes where I pushed myself to the max. I've always prided myself on having strong personal drive, as my father taught me that work ethic is a gift from God. However, was accumulating mountains of stress really part of His plan?

When the dessert was being served, I felt a strange sensation. My arms felt tingly. Sensation shifted into pain in my chest and neck. I started feeling numbness throughout my body, and my forehead and neck were suddenly drenched in sweat. I looked down and my light blue golf shirt was soaking wet on my chest. At first, I thought it was a reaction to the food—maybe this was food poisoning. My next thought was that I was having a heart attack. Both of my grandfathers had passed away from a heart attack and a stroke in their 60s. I thought, "Wow, mine might be coming early."

"Dad, what's going on?" My son Jayce noticed my physical distress and assisted me to the restroom. As we walked across the dining room, I started to lose my sight. I thought, "Get to the restroom before you collapse." I pushed open the restroom door and fell forward, literally crawling to the bathroom stall. I put my head between my knees to resist passing out.

One pronounced thought came to mind: "I can't believe I'm going to die at Mama's Fish House."

It's almost humorous now, but at the time, I was in fear and distress. My son offered me wet towels, and I slowly began to recover.

Later, in the emergency room, I learned that it was not a heart attack but rather a full-blown anxiety attack. How could this be? I was in good shape and on a blissful tropical vacation with my family. I learned that when we finally let our defenses down after a stressful time, our bodies play catch-up and react.

The nurse said something that would forever change my thinking: "Steve, I think it's time for you to rethink and recalibrate how you are living. You need to reset your physical and emotional batteries. Get a full physical and then put a plan in motion for a sustainable pace."

# CASE STUDY: DR. BETH FRATES

Elizabeth "Beth" Pegg Frates, MD, has been a pioneer in lifestyle medicine education since 1996. She has been on faculty at Harvard Medical School and earned several 'Excellence in Teaching Awards' for her work in multiple preclinical courses, including "The Human Central Nervous System" and "Behavior, Musculoskeletal System, and Nutrition."

Most recently, Dr. Beth created a course on lifestyle medicine for the Harvard Extension School. Her syllabus has been adopted by the American College of Lifestyle Medicine. In October 2018, she co-authored a book titled "The Lifestyle Medicine Handbook: An Introduction to the Power of Healthy Habits," which is ranked 50 out of 100 in the category of Best Medical Books Ever by Book Authority.

It's surprising to learn that medicine was not her initial trajectory. When she was 18 years old, she enrolled at Harvard College to pursue a degree in economics with a plan to work in her family's financial firm. That same year, her father, Don Pegg, suffered a heart attack and stroke at 52, leaving him paralyzed on his left side. Thankfully, he made a complete recovery and, subsequently, a complete lifestyle change.

Don Pegg was genetically predisposed to heart disease. It was his lifestyle, however, that triggered the event. He was driven. He woke at 5 am and worked until 11 pm. Before he went to sleep, he snacked on convenience foods while creating task lists for the following day. Even in Don's downtime, work continued to fill his thoughts. His work ethic resulted in incredible production with the accompanying financial success.

# PROFESSIONAL BUCKET

Don put everything into his work. He had a full professional bucket! But he was physically, emotionally, relationally, and soulfully drained. He didn't realize he was running on empty until the stroke revealed the imbalance. Don was fortunate to get a second chance, and he embraced a change of pace.

As Don recovered and reinvented his life, his daughter Beth shifted her career trajectory. She dove into the developing field of lifestyle medicine with the goal of helping others adopt and sustain healthy habits. She observed that, just like her father, many high performers work smart and *fast* but not smart and *healthy*.

Beth graduated magna cum laude from Harvard College, majoring in psychology and biology. Later, she graduated from Stanford Medical School. After completing her residency at Harvard Medical School, she made it her mission to educate others. As of this time, Dr. Beth has created science-based programs through clinical research, focused on six specific areas:

1. Exercise

2. Nutrition

3. Sleep

4. Stress Resiliency

5. Social Connections

6.  Moderation or Elimination of Substances

## YOU CAN FIT IT IN

What keeps people from being smart *and* healthy? Dr. Beth points out an underlying fear:

> *"Most people know what is healthy. They know these concepts. It's really a lack of prioritization. There's this idea we have: 'I have too much to do already. I can't put that on my plate too. I must be successful at work.' What we don't realize is that we can fit these into our day. This is in your control. It's about prioritizing."*

The fear is that change will be overwhelming and all-encompassing. You don't have to immediately change everything, simply begin to shift. That 3° shift will bring you to a completely different destination.

Dr. Beth finds ways to introduce the six areas into her daily routines by making subtle shifts such as employing 'walking meetings' (which additionally increases out-of-box thinking).

Don Pegg lived another 27 years because he was forced to shift. Not everyone is as fortunate to have a second chance after a heart attack, but everybody has the chance to shift so they can avoid the heart attack in the first place.

## VISION LEAKS

**MIKE:** In 2019, I started working with the CEO of a multinational company. He had started his company more than a decade earlier, and as it grew, he discovered that the core values of the company had become obsolete.

He would need to address the company to introduce a new vision. Working together, we crafted a speech that celebrated the past, confronted the present challenges, and invited his employees into a bright future. It was a great speech.

In parting, I said, "Make sure this isn't the last time you talk about these ideas. Repeat them in all your communication. Create videos, share stories, and work these ideas into your meetings. Don't just suddenly announce the new vision and these values to your employees; but make sure you consistently reinforce it in everything you do."

If we don't keep communicating the vision, then the vision... leaks.


## LOVE LEAKS

We've both had the honor of officiating weddings. We have also sadly watched once-happy couples go through tragic divorces. How does that happen? Nobody stands at the altar thinking, "I look forward to the day we sign for our divorce." And yet, divorce is prevalent.

What happens? How do so many couples eventually come to so much pain and animosity?

One of the many reasons is complacency. One wise counselor remarked, "Even after 25 years of marriage, you have to go back to the things you did at first." This counselor recognized that without effort, romance will leak out from the relationship.

If we don't keep filling our relationships with love, then the feelings of love will... leak.

## EDUCATION LEAKS

Have you helped kids with math? It seems like it would be simple to do, doesn't it? After all, we are adults helping kids do something we mastered long ago. However, unless we have kept our math talents up to date, we have found ourselves looking at the page with symbols and formulas we no longer recognize. Why does that happen? Education leaks.

If we don't practice what we learn, our memory of it will... leak.

## LIFE IS LEAKY

Vision leaks. Romance leaks. Education leaks. Life is leaky.

If we don't keep communicating the vision, then the vision leaks. If we don't keep filling our relationships with love, then the feelings of love will leak. If we don't refresh our knowledge, our memory of what we learned will leak. We are each responsible for five buckets: professional production, physical health, emotions, soul, and relationships. Before you focus on filling and refilling all five buckets of life, take a moment to do a preliminary self-examination. After all, to provide a solution, you must first identify the problem.

What problems do you see or anticipate?

- Where are you leaking?

- What have you neglected?

- What are you missing?

- What leaks do you have in life and leadership?

Many leaders focus on the professional bucket: getting work done, building the business, and creating income. As you read through the remaining four, evaluate the level you're at from 1-10. Begin to consider areas you can start to shift.

As you take personal inventory, be careful not to allow guilt to creep in if you are dismayed with the results. When we mentioned this to Dr. Frates, she emphatically stated, "There is no guilt. In lifestyle medicine, we don't guilt ourselves. We say that happened yesterday, but what do we do *now*?"

### YESTERDAY IS PAST. TODAY IS A PRESENT.

# PHYSICAL BUCKET

Now more than ever, leaders need to practice physical self-leadership. Many leaders prioritize the professional bucket, but your physical bucket is the source of energy, your stress management system, and the determining factor of your true leadership sustainability. Your physical bucket will limit or unlock your leadership potential.

*SUSTAINABILITY IS A LEADERSHIP STRATEGY.*

**STEVE:** I confess that my Mama's Fish House Meltdown was a defining moment. Pastor Rick Warren says, "People don't change when they see the light, they change when they feel the heat." My anxiety attack was a heated moment. I no longer neglect regular and disciplined exercise. I've adopted healthy eating habits, started taking nutritional supplements, and I've been prioritizing quality sleep, rest, and recovery.

Our health is a matter of stewardship. We were put on this planet to serve a purpose greater than ourselves. We use our gifts to serve our families and those we are charged to lead.

As you examine the contents of your physical bucket, be inspired to take action to add to it.

Take glance at these forty extraordinary reasons leaders exercise:

1. Lifts your mood and attitude
2. Improves your memory
3. Builds your self-concept
4. Keeps your brain fit

5. Keeps your body fit and strong

6. Boosts your mental health

7. Strengthens your immune system

8. Reduces stress and anxiety

9. Makes you feel happier

10. Has anti-aging effects

11. Improves skin tone and circulation

12. Improves quality of sleep

13. Helps joint function

14. Improves muscle strength

15. Improves sex drive

16. Lowers urges for addiction

17. Boosts creative memory

18. Helps focus

19. Boosts confidence

20. Improves body image

21. Improves eating habits

22. Increases longevity

23. Strengthens bones

24. Strengthens heart function

25. Improves posture

26. Prevents colds/illness

27. Improves cholesterol levels

28. Lowers blood pressure

29. Lowers risk of cancer

30. Lowers risk of diabetes

31. Fights dementia

32. Eases back pain

33. Reduces feelings of depression

34. Prevents muscle loss

35. Increases energy and stamina
36. Improves balance
37. Improves oxygen supply to cells
38. Improves personal presence
39. Improves quality of life
40. Increases joy in personal relationships

Consider the many factors of physical health: exercise, nutrition, sleep, use of substances, and any medical issues needing attention. If you were to place your overall physical health on a scale of 0 to 10, what rating would you choose? What small shift can you make to increase your rating by one?

Can you employ walking meetings? Could you cut down the amount of alcohol you consume each week? Is there any room for more vegetables on your plate? Is there a health challenge to sign up for in your community?

## EMOTIONAL BUCKET

Our lives are filled with unexpected difficulties, challenges, and adversity. No one will master their emotions 100%, but if we get proactive and practice emotional self-regulation, we can stave off any damaging emotions. To combat the onslaught of today's stressors, we need to be able to respond with humility and resilience. This is only possible when we fill our emotional bucket.

Strong leaders don't allow emotions to run empty, and so they don't become victims of their own feelings. Emotional self-leadership is critical. We either allow emotional hijacking or learn to master our emotions and lead the way.

## RE-CREATE-TIONAL ACTIVITIES

To refill our emotional bucket, we must take time for recreation. Think of recreation as re-create-tional time. This time is not just about having something to pass the time, this is something that rebuilds and restores you. These are not activities you do for the purpose of physical health (though that can be a byproduct), these are activities you do for the joy of the activity itself.

**STEVE:** Following my Hawaiian meltdown, I sought out the counsel of my doctor who asked, "Steve, what do you do for your emotional well-being?" I mentioned working out. She corrected, "That's for your physical well-being. What do you do simply because you like doing it?" It became apparent I was lacking in true recreational time. I wasn't having any fun!

**MIKE:** At the onset of my career, I sought out a mentor. He ran a large company and had a full staff. Seeing my eagerness, he agreed to be my coach on the condition that I read every book he recommended, came prepared to our monthly meeting, and acted on his advice. I agreed and committed to his counsel. After working together for a few months he noted that I worked nearly every day of the week, and so he asked, "Mike, what are your hobbies?"

I stared at him, unable to respond. "What do you read for fun? Where do you go on your days off? Do you watch TV?" My silence gave him the answer he was looking for. During that season, I exercised, I studied, and I worked two jobs. That was my life.

"Mike, when I was your age I worked seven days each week until someone told me that I *had* to have a day off. At first, I didn't know what to do, but each Saturday, I began to watch basketball. Watching others play rekindled my own passion to play. Now, when I need to unwind, I go outside and shoot hoops. You need something to do that doesn't feel like you are *doing* something." Taking his advice, I began to get back into rock climbing. Although it also helped fill my physical bucket, I didn't do it for the workout; I did it because I enjoyed it.

The simple pleasures of climbing, walking, biking, gardening, yoga, crafts, swimming, drumming, dancing, solving puzzles, visiting the playground with your kids or grandkids, doing volunteer work, and dog-walking are becoming few and far between.

Today's leaders are held captive to technology. Screen time averages 7-8 hours per day and much of the screen time comes from filling the professional bucket.

Technology has made it hard for today's leaders to find time to unplug and recharge their emotional batteries in order to tap into clarity and wisdom. Researchers from Harvard and the University of Virginia did an experiment in which they gave people a choice to be alone in a room, without anything (device, books, papers, phones), or get an electric shock. 67% of men and 25% of women chose to get an electric shock instead of choosing to be alone and doing nothing.

We'd rather get a bolt of electricity than be alone and quiet!

Many leaders identify as burned out. Most indicate no active recreation on a weekly or bi-weekly basis. Don't become a statistic. Put down the device and pick up an enjoyable hobby. Think, what are some recreational activities you might enjoy? You might start your day with a crossword puzzle. You could take time each weekend to work in your garden. You might commit to playing golf with a friend or a family member.

Start by rating your overall emotional well-being, or ask those close to you to give you feedback. On a scale of 0 to 10, how full is your emotional bucket? Once you are aware of your emotional health, make a plan to pour new energy into your emotional bucket. Select one or two recreational activities and begin to make a 3° shift toward fullness and joy.

## SOULFUL BUCKET

The soul is the incorporeal part of each person. Philosophical, scientific, and religious studies each define it with different words: psyche, consciousness, or spirit. Though the definition varies, the importance remains.

*WE ARE NOT MACHINES, WE ARE HUMAN BEINGS.*

**MIKE:** An executive client recently said in a mastermind group, "If I ignore my spiritual priority for more than three or four days, I sense a lack of compassion and empathy for those I lead.

I quickly shift from servant leadership to self-serving leadership."

Filling your soulful bucket adds incredible value to your leadership by keeping you balanced and centered. I have learned this and make it a priority to spend some time reading, writing, and praying in the morning.

However, there have been times when I did not prioritize my soul. Such was a season in my twenties. The work of stress, the leakiness of my buckets, and my lack of attention to my overall health led me to a place where my passion and vitality eroded. I was worn out and wrestling with why I was doing what I was doing. I identified with John Mayer's 2001 song, *Why Georgia:*

> *Cause I wonder sometimes*
> *About the outcome*
> *Of a still verdictless life*
>
> *Am I living it right?*
> *Am I living it right?*
> *Am I living it right?*
> *Why, why Georgia, why?*
>
> *I rent a room and I fill the spaces with*
> *Wood in places to make it feel like home*
> *But all I feel's alone*
> It might be a quarter life crisis
> Or just the stirring in my soul

Noticing that I was experiencing my own *quarter life crisis* and a *stirring in my soul*, I forced myself to take a weekend retreat.

I drove to a mountain cabin and made a pact with myself to go without talking and eating for twenty-four hours. I walked through the woods. I journaled my thoughts. I sat down in the dirt. I felt... weird. But it was a good sort of weird. I sat there, staring at an ant (meanwhile, the ant ignored me).

Then it happened. Hungry, silent, and rested, I had the most transcendent experience of my life. I was looking down on myself from miles above, seeing myself watching the ant. In that moment, I experienced peace. I was present. I was at rest. Abstaining from speaking and eating gave me clarity. The act of creating space for my soul restored, renewed, and reconnected my soul.

The next day, I drove back home, recharged, and was able to re-engage in more meaningful work. That soulful moment taught me to create space to rest and reflect.

**STEVE:** About five years ago, I recognized a need for more soulful time. I often walked outdoors on the days I wasn't traveling or heavily scheduled with coaching calls. I recalled a Native American Prayer on these walks:

> *What can I appreciate in front of me?*
> *What can I appreciate to my left and right?*
> *What can I appreciate behind me?*
> *What can I appreciate above me?*
> *What can I appreciate within me?*

On those walks, I'd notice the bright path, a colorful leaf, a bright green fern, a sun beam, a rolling cloud above me, and the heartbeat within me. I enjoyed a soulful moment. I was reminded that I'm not a robot, but rather a complex, sensitive, and soulful person.

What are soulful disciplines from your past that may need to be rekindled, reinforced, and reintroduced into your life? What new soulful pursuits interest you?

What are some of your soulful rechargers?

- Quiet music in the early mornings
- A well-worn journal with reflections
- A book of inspiration and wisdom
- Intermittent fasting
- Solitude or perhaps the practice of meditation
- Walks for thinking time
- The Serenity prayer

Your soulful time should be authentic and personal. Don't neglect it or you'll lead a busy yet barren life. Before you move on to the next bucket, take inventory of your soul. On a scale of 0 to 10, how full is your soul?

## RELATIONAL BUCKET

**MIKE:** I'm privileged to hear many personal stories after speaking at events. These stories inspire me and help me understand my audience.

After I stepped down from the stage at an event, a man introduced himself to me. He was the regional director of a well-regarded manufacturing company. After brief pleasantries, I asked him what was on his mind. He paused for an extended moment, and then answered honestly, "I'm lonely."

His answer surprised me. He was a well-liked, influential, and wealthy businessman.

He said he had friends at the company, but he didn't have significant friendships outside of work. Meanwhile, his wife was pushing for a divorce. His son was a busy teenager who didn't have time for his dad. This man had wealth, recognition, and respect, but he didn't have anyone to share it with. He was alone.

This is not an unusual story. Many people feel isolated.

How about you? How full is your relational bucket? Do you have people you connect with on an emotional and soulful level? Do you have someone who knows you?

Your team, co-workers, and colleagues also hunger for meaningful relationships. In fact, one Gallup poll found that companies suffer financially when they don't create an atmosphere where friendships are valued.

It turns out that filling up the relationship bucket overflows into the professional bucket (and others).

# MAKE ROOM FOR RELATIONSHIPS

Patrick Lencioni of The Table Group is the pioneer of the organizational health movement. He coaches team members to make connections. He asks employees to pair up with someone they don't know beyond the work environment, and gives them four questions to ask each other:

- Where were you born and raised?

- How many siblings do you have?

- Where are you in the birth order?

- What is something unique and challenging about your childhood?

As individuals open up to each other, the walls come down, deeper connection is built, and relational buckets begin to fill.

As leaders, it is easy to focus on work tactics and strategies. However, a compassionate and relational leader will often ask different types of questions:

- Share a personal and professional high and low moment you've experienced recently.

- Who do you enjoy working with, and why?

- What can I do for you?

- How are *you*?

Bob Burg, co-author of *Go-Giver,* wisely says, "The most valuable gift you have to offer is yourself," and "Your influence is determined by how abundantly you place other people's interests first." Be the type of leader who creates space for relationships instead of just systems for revenue.

## RELATIONSHIP EXPERT

Shasta Nelson is a leading expert on friendship and healthy relationships. She is the creator of a global community, a keynote speaker, the author of several books, and a popular media resource.

In her book, *The Business of Friendship: Making the Most of Our Relationships Where We Spend Most of Our Time,* Nelson asks, "How can we make friendships the healthiest they can be—both for the sake of the employee and the mission of the company?"

The answer isn't to discourage friendships. It is to teach healthy relationship skills that will benefit the entire workforce.

Our relationships say more about our health, happiness, longevity, and personal growth than any other factor. The lack of friendship can damage our health more than smoking, obesity, or being a life-long alcoholic does. Meanwhile, the presence of healthy relationships can buffer our bodies from absorbing the impact of stress, inspire us to be more of who we are, and leave us with what we crave most: belonging. No matter how you slice it, we all crave belonging. We need it for our mental and emotional well-being. It's also not the quantity of relationships, but rather the quality, that matters. In our disconnected digital world, the relational bucket may be the key to vital health and the perfect stress antidote.

Gauge the quality of your relationships. On a scale of 0 to 10, how are you relating to others?

Once you know your starting point, consider which actions you can take to begin your 3° shift toward filling your relational bucket:

- How can you connect more sincerely with your family?

- How can you communicate more freely with your partner?

- How can you build more and deeper friendships?

## LEAKY BUCKET THEORY

In 1988, Andrew Ehrenberg noted the marketing trend employed by countless companies which was focused on getting *more* customers instead of preventing the loss of their current customers. He called this the "leaky bucket" syndrome. Soon after Ehrenberg defined the syndrome, customer retention became a key marketing strategy. Due to his influence, businesses began to focus on the lifetime value of existing customers instead of the mere acquisition of new customers.

As we discuss our physical, emotional, soulful, and relational buckets, it can be easy to fall into that pre-1988 mindset: 'I just need to get *more* in my bucket'.

But before we begin trying to refill the buckets, it is crucial to first patch up the holes. Start by asking yourself why it is empty:

Where am I low? What have I lost? Why did I lose it?

## CASE STUDY (PART 2): DR. BETH FRATES

At the end of our interview, we asked Dr. Beth: What do *you* fear?

After a pause, Dr. Beth responded: "I think my fear is that I won't reach high enough. I fear that I won't pursue something key that will amplify my message… the thing that people keep telling me would help the nation and would help the world."

Dr. Beth's work relates directly to her fear. She knows the need for a centered, balanced life. She also knows that the world *needs* her work and leadership.

What do you do when your fear directly faces your leadership? *You shift.*

Challenged by some of her students to do *more* and to share *more*, she has been steadily using social media and looking for strategic partnerships. To use the guiding principle of this book, Dr. Beth has employed a subtle 3° shift by doing small actions over a long period of time, instead of overwhelming her schedule all at once.

She has realized what Bill Gates so aptly stated: "Most people overestimate what they can do in one year and underestimate what they can do in ten years."

Learn more about Dr. Beth Frate's work at
www.bethfratesmd.com
and follow her on Twitter @BethFratesMD.

## SHIFTING TOWARD A MORE CENTERED LIFE

When it comes to *performance*, you don't need to be a "well-rounded" leader. You only need to be excellent in a few areas and then trust your team to lead well in the other areas, exhibiting their own strengths.

Bringing a level two weakness up to a level four won't help that much. Instead, bring your level seven strength up to a level nine or ten. Then hire other eight, nines, and tens where you are weak.

When it comes to leadership *performance*, don't be well-balanced, be strategic.

When it comes to *personal health*, it is strategic to be balanced.

You are a symbiotic being, so your social connections, physical health, emotional intelligence, soulful interior, and capacity for professional production flow into each other. Our buckets are not individually contained; they open up into each other. The buckets of your life need to find balance among themselves.

# BUILD RESILIENCE

Janelle Cronk is a Resilience Training Specialist Master of the United States Air Force. She's trained first responders and also conducted trainings at law enforcement agencies, including the FBI National Academy Association.

Cronk tells us, "Resilience is your ability to adapt well and recover quickly after stress, trauma, or tragedy. If you build resilience *strategies* into your leadership core, you'll be better able to maintain poise and a healthy level of physical and psychological wellness in the face of challenges. If you're less resilient, you're more likely to dwell on problems, feel overwhelmed, use unhealthy coping tactics to handle stress, and develop anxiety and depression."

Cronk also works with leaders to build resilience in the 'core-four' buckets: mental, physical, social, and spiritual. Her passion and goal is to help leaders improve their quality of life and decrease their stress and anxiety: something each of us needs for sustainability.

Embrace the wisdom and strategy of Janelle Cronk, Beth Frates, and others from this book. Begin to shift away from solely working smart, and toward smart *and* healthy.

# STRATEGICALLY SHIFT WITH THE BALANCE WHEEL

### IDENTIFY THE LEVELS

To shift from smart to *smart and healthy*, revisit the pages above and identify the levels of each bucket on a scale of 0 to 10 (on the wheel below, the center is 0 and the edge is 10).

____ Professional
____ Physical
____ Emotional
____ Soulful
____ Relational

### VISUALIZE YOUR BALANCE

Mark the level on the wheel in each corresponding bucket, and draw a line across. You may choose to color the area up to the level you identified, or scratch it in with a pen or pencil.

### CHECK YOUR OVERALL HEALTH

When all five parts of the wheel are complete, check the balance by considering how well your wheel would roll with the current level (for example, imagine a wheel with Professional-9, Physical-8, Emotional-8, Soulful-6, Relational-2. Such a wheel would barely be able to roll.)

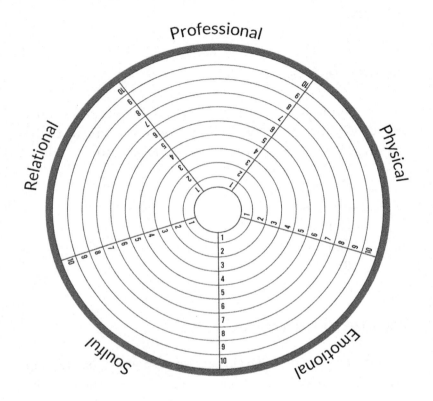

To download a PDF version go to
https://www.nofearworkshop.com/balance

## Use this visual to direct you to create a plan of action:

**8 to 10:**

You are proficient-to-full in this category. You'll want to keep an eye out for the "leaky bucket" syndrome and ensure that this bucket is well-maintained.

**5 to 7:**

Although you are not fully drained, you realize you are lacking in this area. There is significant room for growth.

**1 to 4:**

This is an urgent area needing your focus! Develop a plan to patch holes and fill this bucket. Why do you think your level is so low in this area?

The balance wheel offers you a visual representation of the imbalances in your life. It is simply information organized in a manner to guide you toward creating a more balanced lifestyle as you shift to become smart and healthy.

Which category should you focus on first?

What is one step you can do today to patch up an area?

*Leadership is not something you do to people, it is something you do for people.*

—Ken Blanchard

*It's not where you start but where you finish that counts.*

—Zig Ziglar

## SEVENTH SHIFT:
# FROM FAST TO FINISHING

Many hopeful leaders are in a rush. They're scrambling up the ladder, leaping from promotion to promotion, working endless hours, and attempting to move mountains quickly. They're constantly striving to outperform others.

As we have each learned leadership, we have naively assumed that to become a better leader means to be fast, perform formidable tasks, be recognized as experts in our field, move mountains, transform organizations, and save lives from meaningless work... after all, the world needs help *now!*

The common assumption for both of us was the need to move at lightning speed. Leadership felt like a 100-meter dash. We needed to run fast and outperform the others!

Then, a strange thing occurred. We realized we had been thinking small and selfishly. We had slid into the cultural norm of instant gratification and were focusing too much on sheer performance: streamlined travel, back-to-back engagements, and then quickly moving to the next event.

In our own discovery and timing, we found it was *not* about going fast, up, and to the right. We realized that each day, in fact, holds a new opportunity to commit to finishing *that* day well and make small 3° differences in us and in those around us.

## A BETTER WAY TO LIVE AND LEAD

Leadership isn't about impressing anyone. It's about lifting others up with understanding and empathy. It's about listening. It's about saying, "Thank you." It's about being present with the people we influence.

In the bestselling book *Go-Giver*, co-authors Bob Burg and John David Mann write,

"People, remember this: no matter what your training, no matter what your skills, no matter what area you're in, *you* are your most important commodity. The most valuable gift you have to offer is *you*."

When we live and lead as though we're racing in a back-to-back 100-meter dash, we may win lots of medals, but we *will* miss out on making meaningful memories.

Consider the haunting words of *Cats in the Cradle* by Harry Chapin:

> *My child arrived just the other day*
> *He came to the world in the usual way*
> *But there were planes to catch and bills to pay*
> *He learned to walk while I was away*
> *And he was talkin' 'fore I knew it, and as he grew*
> *He'd say "I'm gonna be like you dad*
> *You know I'm gonna be like you"*

*And the cat's in the cradle and the silver spoon*
*Little boy blue and the man on the moon*
*When you comin' home dad?*
*I don't know when, but we'll get together then son*
*You know we'll have a good time then*

*My son turned ten just the other day*
*He said, "Thanks for the ball, Dad, come on let's play*
*Can you teach me to throw", I said "Not today*
*I got a lot to do", he said, "That's ok"*
*And he walked away but his smile never dimmed*
*And said, "I'm gonna be like him, yeah*
*You know I'm gonna be like him"…*

*I've long since retired, my son's moved away*
*I called him up just the other day*
*I said, "I'd like to see you if you don't mind"*
*He said, "I'd love to, Dad, if I can find the time*
*You see my new job's a hassle and kids have the flu*
*But it's sure nice talking to you, Dad*
*It's been sure nice talking to you"*

*And as I hung up the phone it occurred to me*
*He'd grown up just like me*
*My boy was just like me*

Leadership is not about how fast we can go, but how well we can finish. To finish well, we must take a break. We must pause to think about the destination our current course will lead to if left unchanged. In the case of *Cats in the Cradle*, the parent worked hard and fast and, in the end, arrived at a destination he didn't desire.

To shift from running fast to finishing well, we must stop to ask ourselves, "What destination are we trying to arrive at?"

## WHEN TIME STANDS STILL

**MIKE:** The phone call interrupted my busy evening schedule. "Mike, they are heading to the hospital. They don't know if Karen will live."

When you get a call like that, it changes what's important in an instant. Unfortunately, I have had a few of those calls in my lifetime. Each one left me feeling shaken and reminded me to slow down.

I was 25 years old when I learned that my mom was killed in a car accident. After she died, time slowed to a crawl. Everything that was urgent suddenly became less pressing. My unanswered emails didn't bother me. I leaned into time with my family and with close friends. My work was gracious and allowed me the time and space to do… nothing. After all, there was nothing I could really do. All I could *do* was miss her. Fifteen years later, I still miss my mom.

Once time began to heal the wounds, and I was able to process the loss, my life started to pick up again. Gradually, I found myself returning to my normal, fast-paced life.

Ten years later, I received the call about Karen. Karen was someone else's mom, and a dear friend.

I met Karen's husband Duane at the hospital and was asked to stand with him in the emergency room where they worked to resuscitate his wife. Time stood still as they brought her back, lost her, and brought her back again.

The doctor finally recommended that should her heart stop one more time, it would be time to let her go. We were heartbroken and hopeful. Then Karen's heart stopped, and we helplessly watched as she took her last breath.

Tears come to me as I remember standing there with Duane. He lost the love of his life after being married to her for forty-five years. Slowly, tearfully, Duane tucked her in her hospital bed sheets and then leaned over and kissed her on the forehead. With gratitude and strength, he expressed his love and stated, "Thank you for a wonderful life."

## THANK YOU FOR A WONDERFUL LIFE

Karen passed from this life to the next on February 6, 2017. The hospital waiting room was filled with family. Soon after, her friends filled the church to celebrate her life. Young and old alike came to pay their respects and remember the mother, friend, family member, teacher, co-worker, and leader that Karen had been to the people around her.

*WHEN YOU GO FAST, YOU MIGHT MISS THE OPPORTUNITIES THAT LAST.*

Every time I remember Duane's final words to Karen, life slows down, and I'm reminded of what's truly important.

"Thank you for a wonderful life."

True leadership and success are really just about being loved and respected by those closest to you.

We invite you to shift your thinking. Instead of focusing on how fast you can go, look further ahead. Think about how you want to finish the journey, and who you want to finish it with.

## LESSONS FROM EMBARRASSING MOMENTS

**STEVE:** I've been going to the same grocery store for over twenty years. I know all the store clerks. A few years ago, I was in a hurry and shopping quickly. I needed a few items for a barbeque. As I waited in line to check out, I realized I didn't recognize the cashier; she was new. She was working at a snail's pace.

I huffed and puffed, as the person in front of me looked back, rolling their eyes as if to say, "Can you believe this slowpoke?" When it was finally my turn, I slid my cart up as fast as I could and said, "Looks like you need a little more training before they throw you out here!"

I'm not proud of this. To this day, my comment grieves and embarrasses me.

She paused, then said, "Sir, you are right. This is all new to me. I used to be a stay-at-home mom. My husband was recently killed in an accident and I'm working for the first time."

In an instant, I could see there was darkness in my heart. Why was I so rude? Why was I in such a rush?

"I am so sorry. Forget about what I just said. You are doing just fine, and what I said was wrong. I'm so sorry for your loss." The words seemed empty, although they were sincere.

This was a reminder that I needed to do some work within myself before focusing on outward accomplishments.

"Fast to finishing" is about choosing to lead every day. Leading is not about what we gain from others, but about what others gain from us, as well. This means we have to be prepared to sacrifice some of our well-intended deadlines, to slow down our pace at times. We must remember that we are not machines; we are human beings. The people we serve and come into contact with are human beings, too, with hearts, souls, and feelings.

## FINISH WELL

A few years back, I was working with a highly-recognized leader who stated, "It is not my job to be liked, it's my job to get things done!"

That all sounded good until he had a life-altering battle with cancer. When he finally came back to work after weeks of chemotherapy treatments, his once-bold bravado had disappeared.

"For far too long, I've been this cutthroat king of executing plans, at all costs. My team doesn't care for me, and quite frankly, I've alienated my wife, children, and a lot of business friends. I've been rethinking how I treat people."

When confronted with death, the once-fast leader didn't just receive chemotherapy treatments, but also treatments for the heart and soul. Slowing down to confront the threat of death forced him to think through how he would finish.

How about you?

How will you finish?

The way you conduct yourself each and every day will be a part of your legacy. Success in leadership is not measured only in numbers and profit margins. We have a responsibility to leave this world better than we found it.

## HELPING OTHERS FINISH WELL

What can you *give* to others?

| | | |
|---|---|---|
| Extra Support | Acceptance | Empathy |
| Leads & Referrals | Passion | Tried & Tested Techniques |
| Encouragement | Personal Sacrifice | Respect |
| Innovation | Good Advice | Feedback |
| Vision | Protection | The Benefit of the Doubt |

## GREATER THAN YOU REALIZE

Your influence, impact, and inspiration are greater than you realize.

When you choose to lead every day with your team, customers, and family, you are choosing significant impact over short-term measures of success. All great and lasting leaders ultimately have the chance to be human and bring out the best in others. People will come away from you feeling better about themselves and their situation.

As our mentor and author of numerous leadership books, John Maxwell said, "It has been said that there are two kinds of people in life: those who make things happen and those who wonder what happened. People who don't know how to make things happen for themselves won't know how to make things happen for others. What you do with the future means the difference between leaving a track record and leaving a legacy."

## YOUR LEGACY STORY STARTS TODAY

Shifting from fast to finishing isn't about wishful thinking. It is about determination. Your legacy is being created today, right now, this very minute. The legacy you leave your spouse, children, teammates, and clients you serve is through the life you lead. We lead our lives daily. How you treat others, how you speak to others, the decisions you make, the actions you take today... they tell your story.

Our stories are written on the hearts of others. It's the sum of everything you do that matters most, not one big crescendo at the end of your career as you retire into the sunset. For all the talk about the future, the most important leadership actions are the ones you take today! You just never know whose life you will touch or what that encounter might initiate.

*OUR LEGACY IS WRITTEN ON THE HEARTS OF OTHERS.*

## WHAT WILL IT LOOK LIKE?

Mike Kami is a world-renowned strategic planning consultant. Kami asks leaders:

- How can you be most useful?

- Where should you invest your talents, time, and treasure?

- What are the values that give purpose to your life?

- What is your overarching vision that shapes your decisions?

- Where are you going?

- How will you get there?

## CASE STUDY: ROB WAGGENER

**STEVE:** Rob Waggener is CEO and Chairman of Promises Behavior Health, a fully accredited drug, rehabilitation, and mental health treatment center with many locations across the United States.

I was privileged to partner with Rob and his leadership team for an offsite retreat. Rob and I had just ordered a meal and Rob posed a great question: "Steve, what do you think is the most important trait of an influential leader?"

My mind raced. Is it integrity? Is it vision? Empowerment? Self-awareness? Trust?

I answered, "Rob, I'd be curious to hear your thoughts."

Rob said, "It's humility. I've done a lot of thinking about this and I believe humility is at the core of all great leadership. It keeps your ego in check... and with humility, a leader works in service to others."

We were interrupted by a loud thud, and Rob jumped to his feet. A woman at the table behind us had collapsed to the floor. Within seconds, Rob was by her side.

She was nearly unconscious. Someone said, "I think she is having a seizure."

"No, she is choking!" Rob lifted the woman up and proceeded to perform the Heimlich Maneuver. With two first thrusts, a piece of food popped out of her mouth, and the woman was able to breathe again.

Everyone was holding their breath! Rob assisted her back to her chair. She was shaken, but thankful.

## EGO VS LOVE

It's no surprise that Rob Waggener is a hero. He's a humble servant to others.

Rob starts his day slowly in solitude, reflection, and meditation. Before work clamors for his attention, he works to center himself spiritually. He believes that fear and gratitude cannot occupy the same space, and so he lives his life in gratitude.

Additionally, Rob practices pausing before speaking. He doesn't want to rush his way into a wrong message.

He believes that we lead from either ego or love. Ego is driven by fear and insecurity; love always has the right motivation.

Rob leads his organization with humility and with one simple promise: to help his clients find strength, inspiration, and hope to begin a new life in recovery.

Rob leads with no fear.

## SHIFT

Shifting from fast to finishing has some remarkable benefits. People will sense your sincerity and centeredness.

If you are in sales, you'll attract greater connection and loyalty.

If you are an entrepreneur, you'll generate better results because people will trust your intentions.

If you lead a team, people will work hard for you and do it with heart and soul because they know you care for them deeply. Loyalty is not something a boss can demand, it's something people choose to grant to a person who has earned it.

What are your team's aspirations, fears, and ideals? How can you shift to meeting the needs of your team and showing a deeper level of respect? How can you shift to having a more genuine connection with those you serve?

We will all be remembered for something. What will others say about you when you're no longer around? What shift can you make now to ensure a lasting legacy of purpose?

*Be faithful in small things because it is in them that your strength rises.*

—Mother Teresa


*Patience, persistence, and perspiration make an unbeatable combination of success.*

—Napoleon Hill

# CONCLUSION

We both have a small "post-it note" on our desks. It reads: 1440.

1440. That's how many minutes we get, each and every day, to lead our lives and leave our legacies. It's a simple reminder to invest time in meaningful work and purposeful relationships.

We've found we need to focus on our energy. That's the one thing we can influence most.

In *The Power of Full Engagement,* authors Jim Loehr and Tony Schwartz write:

*"Energy, not time, is the fundamental currency of high performance."* They go on to explain, *"The ultimate measure of our lives is not how much time we spend on the planet, but rather how much energy we invest in the time we have."*

Their premise is simple: Performance, health, and happiness are improved through the skillful management of energy. The number of hours in a day is fixed, but the quantity and quality of energy can be cultivated. It is our most precious resource.

The more we take responsibility for the energy we bring to the world, the more empowered and productive we become. The more we blame others or external circumstances, the more negative and compromised our energy is going to be.

People who strive boldly and reach their potential do not sit back and wait for things to happen. They identify limiting beliefs and fears that hold them back. They expose those beliefs to a new paradigm of energy and focus. They reverse limiting behaviors that erode their goals and dreams.

They shift.

High performing leaders start by working on themselves.

High-performing leaders also start one step at a time.

# JUST 3°

Transformation is possible. With 3° shifts, small, incremental, and intentional actions, you will achieve real and lasting results.

### *First Shift:* **From Victim to Leader**
Rid yourself of a victim mindset, victim self-talk, and victim vocabulary.

### *Second Shift:* **From Unaware to Self-aware**
Discover your blind spots and understand how others perceive your leadership.

### *Third Shift:* **From Black and White to High-Definition**
Clarify your personal vision for life and professional vision for leadership.

### *Fourth Shift:* **From Insecure to Confident**

Move from dwelling on your deficiencies to focusing on what you can give.

### *Fifth Shift:* **From Activity to Accomplishment**

Focus on the most valuable and profitable priorities, not checking things off a list for instant gratification.

### *Sixth Shift:* **From Smart to Smart AND Healthy**

Discover how balance in life benefits work, relationships, health, and everything else.

### *Seventh Shift:* **From Fast to Finishing**

Dream about how to build your legacy, not just your resume.

These seven shifts, combined with consistent and positive action, will create the lasting legacy you desire and lead you to your desired destination.

## "MIRACULOUS" DESTINATIONS

**MIKE:** Rachel Richards, the author of a bestselling book on financial management, came to me as a communication client. Agents had begun to reach out to her for keynotes, and she needed help preparing for media appearances.

It was while I coached Rachel that I felt inspired to write my first book, *Speak With No Fear.* I asked her for advice about writing.

"Do it one day at a time," she replied.

Every day, Rachel worked on her book. When she completed her first book, she worked on promoting it every day. Then she began to work on her second book. For two years, she worked on *Passive Income, Aggressive Retirement*. She published her book in 2019.

Ultimately, Rachel Richards retired at the age of 27.

When she first started writing at 23, she didn't know what exact destination she would end up at. She just knew that she needed to make a shift, one day at a time.

What shift will you begin to make one day at a time?

## "MIRACULOUS" DECISIONS

Kevin James stars as Albert Brennaman in the movie *Hitch*. Kevin's character, Albert, is desperately in love with Allegra Cole, a beautiful woman who works with his financial firm for her financial investment. To Allegra, Albert is just another man in a black suit who manages her vast wealth. Albert would have continued going by unnoticed had he not decided to do something differently.

Albert seeks out a coach in Will Smith's character, Alex "Hitch" Hitchens. In the movie, Hitch leads Albert to do something different: Hitch challenges Albert to stand out, overcome his fears, and take a risk.

And so Albert Brennaman takes action, faces his fears, and boldly speaks out. He confronts his boss, challenges Allegra to take action, and quits his job.

No, we're not saying you need to quit your job. We're saying:

### YOU NEED AN ALBERT BRENNAMAN MOMENT!

After all, if you always do what you've always done, you will get what you've always got.

And we know that if you've picked up this book and read till this point, the final section, you have what it takes to make those 3° shifts, create a legacy that means something, and lead with no fear.

You've got it in you.

*Motivation is what gets you started. Habit is what keeps you going.*

—John Rohn

*So please ask yourself, what would I do if I weren't afraid? And then go do it.*

—Sheryl Sandberg

# YOUR 90-DAY PLAN TO A-C-T

Checking in with your 90-day action plan regularly will shift your leadership influence, impact, and inspiration into actionable results. Instead of wasting time on trivial activities that fail to move you toward your purpose-driven goals and pursuits, focus on daily, weekly, monthly, and quarterly shifts. Concentrate on your MVP (most valuable and profitable) goals that connect you to your passion, purpose, and pursuits and your life will shift to significance and lasting leadership success.

*To download a 90-day PDF visit*
https://www.nofearworkshop.com/90-day

With each 90-day action plan worksheet you complete, don't forget to fill in the appropriate date, month, and quarter for your action plans. Feel free to repeat and adjust as often as you'd like.

**The Seven Shifts are:**

1.  Victim to Leader

2.  Unaware to Aware

3.  From Black & White to HD

4.  Insecure to Confident

5. Activity to Accomplishment

6. Smart to Smart & Healthy

7. Fast to Finishing

# Your Daily/Weekly Action Plan

1. Select one shift to focus on this day and/or week:

2. List the MVP (*Most Valuable and Profitable*) accomplishments you must complete this week:

3. List projects to work on one step at a time (at a minimum) each day:

4. Note one fear to identify and eliminate this week:

5. List words, affirmations, and leadership vocabulary you will speak this week:

6. Outline one SMART (*Specific, Measurable, Attainable, Relevant, and Timebound*) goal for your professional career this week:

# Your 90-Day (Quarterly) Action Plan

1. Select three (3) shifts to focus on this quarter:

   1.

   2.

   3.

2. Outline three (3) MVP accomplishments you'd like to accomplish this quarter:

   1.

   2.

   3.

3. What are your top five (5) projects for this quarter?

   1.

   2.

   3.

   4.

   5.

4. Reflect to identify two (2) fears you'd like to eliminate this quarter:

    1.

    2.

5. What words of affirmation and leadership vocabulary would you like to speak this quarter?

6. Select three (3) SMART goals to set professionally this quarter:

    1.

    2.

    3.

# Your Annual Reflect and Review

1. What is your purpose and vision for your life and leadership?

2. What is your vision for your business or role at work?

3. What are your top five (5) values for life and leadership?

1.

2.

3.

4.

5.

4. Outline your top five (5) personal goals for this year:

    1.

    2.

    3.

    4.

    5.

5. Select and note three (3) top shifts for this year:

    1.

    2.

    3.

6. What new developing skills would you like to focus on this year?

7. What are your top 20 MVP contacts to make this year?

    1.

    2.

    3.

4.

5.

6.

7.

8.

9.

10.

11.

12.

13.

14.

15.

16.

17.

18.

19.

20.

*The below space is for your notes, ideas, and inspiration (mentors and coaching).*

# MAKE SURE TO A-C-T

We titled this book: *Lead With No Fear: Your 90-day Leadership Shift from Worry, Insecurity, and Self-doubt to Inspiration, Clarity, and Confidence.*

In order for you to maximize this claim, you must A-C-T: Apply, Change, Transfer.

## PARTICIPATE IN YOUR OWN RESCUE

**STEVE:** During my transforming experience of rafting and kayaking with burn survivors, we traveled many miles, navigating calm waters and turbulent whitewater rapids. During the orientation, the guides warned that there were "no joke" serious rapids ahead, and that we would flip our kayaks from time to time.

The instructions were clear: "As soon as you flip out of your kayak, sit up with your head high, point your feet downstream, use your legs to push off any upcoming rocks, and we will throw you a line with a handle on it. Your responsibility is to grab that line and pull yourself toward us. *You will need to participate in your own rescue!*"

Rescue could not be passive. We had to be active, aggressive, and we had to participate.

As authors and leadership coaches, we've done our best to provide actionable points to lead with no fear. Now, it's time for you to participate and actively engage.

## A—APPLICATION

Over the next 90 days, methodically focus on these seven strategies. Apply a 3° shift and set an actionable goal for the next 90 days.

*WE MAKE OUR HABITS AND OUR HABITS MAKE US.*

Use the content and questions from the chapters to develop your own life motto, mission, or vision.

You may gain inspiration by searching online or by studying sources such as The Four Agreements from David Forster:

1. Always do your best

2. Be impeccable with your words

3. Don't take things personally

4. Don't make assumptions

# C—CHANGE

Courageously change limiting beliefs and behaviors in the next 90 days.

1. Can you identify a limiting *belief* that is holding you back? It could be:

- Lack of education

- Lack of experience or qualification

- Thinking you are too old

- A damaged self-concept from your youth

- A failure in your past seeded doubts and fears

It's time to take that limiting behavior and destroy it. Lean into what scares you, and it will get smaller and smaller. Soon, that once-debilitating belief will disappear.

2. Can you identify a limiting *behavior* that is holding you back? It could be:

- Procrastination

- Negative self-talk

- Eating poorly

- Getting distracted by news or social media

# T—TRANSFER:

Share your shifts with *others*. Don't be like a pond with just one source of water flowing in. The healthiest lakes have a source flowing in and out.

When you transfer knowledge and skills to others, you compound your success.

*"If your actions inspire others to dream more, learn more, do more, and become more, you are a leader."*

—John Quincy Adams

# ACKNOWLEDGMENTS

## ACKNOWLEDGMENTS BY STEVE

When my co-author, Mike Acker, and I sat at Wood's Coffee in Bellevue, Washington to discuss writing *Lead With No Fear,* I had no idea that COVID-19 would soon sweep through our world. I couldn't imagine that Kirkland, Washington, just 20 minutes from where I live outside of Seattle, would register as the national epicenter of the virus. *Lead With No Fear* guided us through this pandemic.

I first want to thank Mike for his dedication and devotion to this book. We cheered one another on to write with the belief that transformational change can occur in 3° shifts and within 90 days!

To my life partner, Julie, who leads fearlessly as my wife and mother to our three adult children, Jenna, Jayce, and Kyle, to their partners Kamran and Cherisse, and to my six grandchildren who keep us all young at heart with our frequent playground visits. You all are my "why" and my driving purpose to "inspire greatness in others."

A special thanks to my executive assistant, Jamie Pennington, who keeps my schedule, communicates with all my clients, arranges travel, orders my day, and typed every word of the chicken scratch I wrote, scanned, and sent her with this book project. You are only as good as your team, and I'm blessed beyond words to have Jamie, Michelle Joyce, Leeann Cannon, Gary Thompson, Brian Jeide, and Caleb Couch in my corner.

To my beloved parents, Tom and Carolyn Gutzler, who first modeled love and leadership to me, while teaching me the value of serving others, of generosity, and servant leadership. To my football coach, Don Matthew, who said, "You don't need to be a captain to be a leader." To my Pastor, Ron Mehl, who said, "Steve, you are a gifted communicator, you need to speak." And to my God, who has chosen to use a flawed man to inspire greatness in others and lead with no fear!

Finally, to our readers: We can lead with courage and clarity. Together, we can change the world!

## ACKNOWLEDGMENTS BY MIKE

In January 2019, someone recommended Steve Gutzler to partner with me on a team event I was organizing. I needed to bring in a new voice, and Steve did an incredible job connecting with us, with incredible content, powerful stories, and a meaningful assignment.

After the event ended, Steve and I discovered that we had a family connection! His daughter and my sister had married brothers. With this extended family connection, similar lines of work, and a great personal connection, we decided to stay in contact. We reconnected just prior to the beginning of the coronavirus pandemic. As cafes closed, we decided to practice what we preach by finding opportunity in obstacles. Our Wood's Cafe idea would become this book. We hope to inspire others.

Working with Steve on this project has been incredible. We've pushed each other, encouraged each other, and brought out the best in each other. I want to thank Steve taking this journey with me. I've become a better person, leader, coach, and author as a result. Thank you!

I heart-fully thank my wife every time I write a book, and I wish to thank her again! She allows me the time in the mornings and evenings to put on my Apple playlist and write. And write. And write. Thank you, Taylor, for your love, your work, and your patience!

A special thank you to Aimée Bruneau, our Lead Coach and Program Concierge at ADVANCE. She came to work with me at the perfect time. She provides incredible coaching, impeccable organization, and she has helped me get this ready to publish.

And thank *you* for entrusting us with your time and energy. We hope that the stories, studies, and principles in this book inspire you to lead with motivation, clarity, and confidence!

# ABOUT THE AUTHORS

## ABOUT STEVE

Steve Gutzler is an on-demand keynote speaker on emotional intelligence and transformational leadership. His principles and practices have inspired audiences around the country. He has partnered with and presented to major global brands and countless fortune-500 companies such as Microsoft, LinkedIn, Spotify, The Ritz Carlton, Seattle Seahawks, Boeing, Kraft Foods, and with federal agencies, law enforcement, hospitals, and technology startups.

He's a husband, father of three children, and grandfather to six grandchildren, who keep him young and a frequent playground visitor.

### IF YOU ARE INTERESTED IN CONTACTING STEVE

for a keynote program, team workshop, or online training:

**EMAIL:** Steve at contact@stevegutzler.com
**WEBSITE:** www.SteveGutzler.com

You can also sign up for Steve's weekly leadership newsletter at:
www.SteveGutzler.com

## ABOUT MIKE

Mike Acker is the CEO of ADVANCE where he leads his growing team on the mission **to turn people's potential into actual** through workshops, communication programs, and executive coaching. His *Speak* and *No Fear* series of books inspire audiences to break through barriers to achieve new levels of success. ADVANCE has partnered with individuals and organizations close to home, and all over the world.

Mike enjoys rock-climbing, wake surfing, skiing, his church, building Legos with his son, and going on dates with his wife, Taylor. Mike believes in the power of prayer, in exercise, journaling, and leaning on his community in order to counter the stress of everyday life.

### IF YOU ARE INTERESTED IN WORKING WITH ADVANCE, please contact.:
info@stepstoadvance.com

### IF YOU WANT TO BOOK MIKE ACKER
for a speaking engagement, please contact:
mike.acker@stepstoadvance.com

### To stay connected visit :
https://subscribe.stepstoadvance.com/me

# BRING **LEAD WITH NO FEAR** TRAINING TO YOUR ORGANIZATION

## DEVELOP LEADERSHIP
## BUILD YOUR TEAM

**OUR SERVICES**
- Conferences
- Offsite Half or Full-day Workshops
- Organizational Assessments and Resources
- 30-minute and 1-hour Virtual Trainings
- Coaching for Keynote Presentations
- Executive and Leadership Coaching

E-mail:

contact@nofearworkshop.com

# BOOK
# STEVE GUTZLER

## DISCOVER THE PROVEN PRINCIPLES AND PRACTICES THAT MAKE LEADERS GREAT AND TEAMS THRIVE

**Steve Gutzler** is an on-demand keynote speaker on emotional intelligence and transformational leadership. His principles and practices have inspired audiences around the nation.

He has partnered and presented with major global brands and countless fortune-500 companies such as Microsoft, LinkedIn, Spotify, The Ritz Carlton, Seattle Seahawks, Boeing, Kraft Foods, US Federal Agencies, Law Enforcement, Hospitals, and technology startups.

contact@stevegutzler.com

# INSPIRE GREATNESS AND BRING OUT YOUR TEAMS BEST

**Steve Gutzler** is a uniquely different speaker. His authentic, inspiring style moves people to action. Steve has spent 25 years coaching, training, and working one on one with Fortune-500 companies and leading organizations such as Microsoft, Kraft Foods, LinkedIn, Spotify, The Ritz Carlton, Seattle Seahawks, Boeing, Federal US Agencies, Hospitals, and technology startups.

His keynote presentations teach today's leaders how to reach their full potential, build unstoppable inner confidence, and achieve sustainable success. He is a recognized expert of emotional intelligence and transformational leadership, and has delivered over 2,500 presentations. Steve's keynotes are a high-energy, motivational experience that will leave audiences inspired and moved to action.

If you are interested in booking Steve Gutzler for a keynote presentation, workshop, or online training, please contact **steve@stevegutzler.com** or visit **www.SteveGutzler.com**. You can also follow Steve on Twitter, Instagram, and Facebook.

*"Steve Gutzler has been an irrefutable 'wow' during our Annual General Managers Conference, as well as our Leadership Team Advances. He has a unique way of bringing energy, authenticity, and actionable takeaways."*

**– Doug Dreher, CEO, The Hotel Group**

# BOOK
# MIKE ACKER

## INCREASE CONFIDENCE, DETERMINE DESTINATIONS, AND TRANSFORM POTENTIAL INTO ACTUAL FOR INDIVIDUALS AND TEAMS.

**Mike Acker** is part of the John Maxwell Team. He is a certified leadership speaker, a gifted storyteller, and award winning Thumbtack Top Pro for event organizers. His presentations are prompted by his extensive personal leadership experience, his international upbringing and education, and his authorization to teach licenced material from leadership guru, John Maxwell.

In addition to speaking, he has trained many executives and teams in their communication and company leadership, including Adobe, Oracle and INOapps, Amazon, Microsoft, MLB, and Silicon Valley Startups. He has served as a speaker coach for TEDx presenters, orators, and politicians.

## contact@mikeacker.com

If you are interested in inviting Mike Acker to speak for your event or coach your team email **contact@mikeacker.com**. He and his coaching team also blog on **www.stepstoadvance.com/blog** and can be found on LinkedIn, Twitter, and Facebook.

*"I have had Mike speak at multiple functions of audiences from 20-500 people, and his ability to connect and motivate diverse groups of people is amazing! I would highly recommend Mike. Additionally, Mike has been a consistent encouragement in my own development. He gives good feedback and practical advice both on the stage and off."*

**– Micah Jaquay,**
**CEO, Praxis Technology**

Made in the USA
Monee, IL
01 November 2021

81220155R00115